This book is exceptional in every way cal depth, spiritual insight, and pasto beautiful landscape of comfort and en....... to cherish. *Consider the Lilies* is a transformational gift that should become a classic.

JOHN MACARTHUR, PASTOR, GRACE COMMUNITY CHURCH

Anxiety, depression, fear, and insecurity plague this generation. We need answers! Jonny Ardavanis has provided us with timeless answers and what I see as one of the most essential resources of our day. I know his background and experience, and I have seen his pastoral heart on display. He is wise beyond his years and has a passion for seeing people set free from the bondage keeping them in chains. This book will point us all back to the character of God and be a trusted resource for years to come.

COSTI W. HINN, TEACHING PASTOR, SHEPHERD'S HOUSE BIBLE CHURCH; FOUNDER AND PRESIDENT, FOR THE GOSPEL

In the last century, cultural observers began to warn about an "age of anxiety." These days, we live in an atmosphere of nearly undiluted anxiety. It's in the air we breathe, and it pervades our entire culture. In this important new book, Jonny Ardavanis points us to God's self-revelation in Scripture as our only escape from the anxiety the world would otherwise press upon us all. He offers biblical counsel grounded in the gospel of Jesus Christ that unapologetically affirms God's power and divine sovereignty.

R. ALBERT MOHLER JR., PRESIDENT AND CENTENNIAL PROFESSOR OF CHRISTIAN THEOLOGY, THE SOUTHERN BAPTIST THEOLOGICAL SEMINARY

We have the mind of Christ, the apostle Paul tells us, so it makes sense that we should think about what Christ tells us to think about. Anxiety is one reason this is easier said than done. *Consider the Lilies* is full of all the reminders you and I tend to forget when we fill our minds with everything but what Christ tells us to meditate on. If you need safeguarding against anxiety, please read this book and "consider the lilies."

GLORIA FURMAN, AUTHOR, *TREASURING CHRIST WHEN YOUR HANDS ARE FULL*

The title of this book immediately brings to mind the words of Jesus, who rebuked the disciples for their fear and worry. After all, if God takes care of the lilies of the field, will he not care for us as well? In this book, Jonny Ardavanis goes directly to the source of our anxiety—namely, our inadequate view of the character of God. It stands to reason that the better we understand the attributes of our heavenly Father, the less anxiety we will have. Read this book to remind yourself that God has already lived your tomorrows!

ERWIN W. LUTZER, PASTOR EMERITUS, MOODY CHURCH, CHICAGO

In a world where anxiety and the pressures of daily life can feel overwhelming, Jonny Ardavanis masterfully guides us to shift our focus from our worries to the steadfast, unchanging character of God. With profound biblical insights and practical applications, he teaches us to anchor our thoughts in the unchanging nature of Jesus Christ. His emphasis on meditating on God's Word, engaging in heartfelt prayer, and building strong relationships has deeply impacted my spiritual journey. His compassionate, pastoral approach provides a lifeline for those yearning for freedom from anxiety and fear. I wholeheartedly recommend this book to anyone looking to deepen their trust in God and experience His perfect peace.

MARK SPENCE, SENIOR VICE PRESIDENT, LIVING WATERS; AUTHOR; TV AND PODCAST HOST, WAY OF THE MASTER

Ours is a culture plagued by crippling fears and anxieties. Few are immune from this epidemic, and that holds true for many Christians. Furthermore, we have turned to the useless escape mechanisms, distractions, and psychological idols of our secular ethos that helped create the problem in the first place. Jonny Ardavanis has seen the devastation firsthand, and he points us to the one and only antidote—clinging to the glorious triune God unveiled in the pages of Scripture. Jonny leads us to find our refuge in the eternal, benevolent, and sovereign God who knows and loves His children.

SCOTT CHRISTENSEN, PASTOR; AUTHOR, WHAT ABOUT FREE WILL? AND DEFEATING EVIL

Jonny Ardavanis beautifully illuminates the profound truth that perfect peace is found in understanding the holy character of God. *Consider the Lilies* is a timely resource for believers seeking solace amid the turmoil of life in a constantly changing world. Johnny reminds us that to know ourselves truly, we must first know who God is, and he exhorts us to let Scripture inform our emotions. He provides invaluable help for the Christian's growth in grace.

CHRIS LARSON, PRESIDENT AND CEO, LIGONIER MINISTRIES

Consider the Lilies is a much-needed, refreshing, and comprehensive look at the antidote to anxiety. Jonny Ardavanis helps us cut through the surface of worry and anxiety and shows us that focusing on the character of God is the pathway to peace.

BRIANNA HARRIS, DEAN OF WOMEN, THE MASTER'S UNIVERSITY

Jonny Ardavanis does not consider anxiety in a simplistic nor overly complicated way. Instead, he approaches it the way Christians need to frame every issue—biblically and in light of the character of God. His pastor's heart and love for the Bible come through clearly. Anyone who struggles with anxiety, or loves someone who does, will be greatly helped by what Jonny has written.

ERIK THOENNES, PhD, PROFESSOR OF THEOLOGY, TALBOT SCHOOL OF THEOLOGY, BIOLA UNIVERSITY; PASTOR, GRACE EVANGELICAL FREE CHURCH, LA MIRADA; AUTHOR, *LIFE'S BIGGEST QUESTIONS*

We live in a day when stress, anxiety, and depression are increasingly the rule rather than the exception. *Consider the Lilies* is not a typical book on anxiety, for it is not man-centered but radically God-centered. By the Spirit's strength, let us shine as lights by showing this dark world that our triune God can indeed provide peace that surpasses all understanding.

JOEL R. BEEKE, CHANCELLOR AND PROFESSOR OF HOMILETICS AND SYSTEMATIC THEOLOGY, PURITAN REFORMED THEOLOGICAL SEMINARY

After a significant trial in my life, I found myself facing something I was unfamiliar with—anxiety and its physiological effects. In that dark time of uncertainty, what kept me not just afloat but thriving was setting my gaze upon the glory of Christ. I am so thankful that Jonny Ardavanis provided this much-needed resource. Not only have I seen the joy of living out these principles in my own life, but I now also have an invaluable resource for counseling and discipling those who struggle with fear, worry, anxiety, and depression. May this book be a balm to your soul.

ERIN COATES, WIFE OF PASTOR JAMES COATES; WOMEN'S MINISTRY DIRECTOR, GRACELIFE CHURCH, EDMONTON

For those who may have accepted anxiety as a given for the modern mind, *Consider the Lilies* proposes a new hope—reachable for the layperson and dripping with deep theological truths.

CHRIS HILKEN, SENIOR PASTOR, COLLEGE AVE. CHURCH, SAN DIEGO

Consider the Lilies

Consider
the
Lilies

Finding
Perfect Peace
in the
Character
of God

Jonny
Ardavanis

ZONDERVAN
BOOKS

ZONDERVAN BOOKS

Consider the Lilies

Copyright © 2024 by Jonny Ardavanis

Published in Grand Rapids, Michigan, by Zondervan. Zondervan is a registered trademark of The Zondervan Corporation, L.L.C., a wholly owned subsidiary of HarperCollins Christian Publishing, Inc.

Requests for information should be addressed to customercare@harpercollins.com.

Zondervan titles may be purchased in bulk for educational, business, fundraising, or sales promotional use. For information, please email SpecialMarkets@Zondervan.com.

Library of Congress Cataloging-in-Publication Data
Names: Ardavanis, Jonny, 1992- author.
Title: Consider the lilies : finding perfect peace in the character of God / Jonny Ardavanis.
Description: Grand Rapids, Michigan : Zondervan, [2024]
Identifiers: LCCN 2024021575 (print) | LCCN 2024021576 (ebook) | ISBN 9780310368243 (softcover) | ISBN 9780310368250 (ebook) | ISBN 9780310368267 (audio)
Subjects: LCSH: Consolation—Religious aspects—Christianity. | Anxiety—Religious aspects—Christianity. | BISAC: RELIGION / Christian Living / Personal Growth | RELIGION / Christian Living / Inspirational
Classification: LCC BV4905.3 .A665 2024 (print) | LCC BV4905.3 (ebook) | DDC 242/.4—dc23/eng/20240605
LC record available at https://lccn.loc.gov/2024021575
LC ebook record available at https://lccn.loc.gov/2024021576

Published in association with the literary agency of Wolgemuth & Associates, Inc.

Cover design: Faceout Studio, Jeff Miller
Cover illustration: MINIMALARTIST / Shutterstock
Interior design: Kristy L. Edwards

Printed in the United States of America

24 25 26 27 28 LBC 6 5 4 3 2

To my girls—
Caity Jean, Lily Jean, and Scottie Joan—
I love you

Contents

Part III: Our Way Forward

Foreword

M any of us are familiar with the words of Jesus that form the title of this wise and helpful book. But can you remember why Jesus thought His exhortation to consider the lilies was so important? He had just told His anxious hearers, "Do not be anxious" (Matthew 6:25 ESV). And this is not the only time He gave the same counsel.

But isn't there something strange about this? You would be unlikely to ace a board exam to be a licensed counselor by giving that answer to the question, "What would you say to someone whose first words to you were, 'I'm struggling with anxiety. I don't seem to be able to master it. Can you help me, please?'" Surely telling an anxiety-ridden person, "Do not be anxious," is a bit like telling a person who has broken their leg that the only cure is walking, isn't it?

And yet this is what Jesus said. Did He fail "Counseling the Anxious 101"? Hardly. What, in fact, He did was acknowledge the reality of anxiety, but then give reasons, offer teaching, and especially reveal the character of our Father God as the way of deliverance from anxiety's paralysis. With gentle arguments and illustrations, Jesus demonstrated that there are bigger and stronger reasons for not being anxious than there are for being anxious. And in doing so, He prescribed a remedy found in knowing the heavenly Father's love,

generous provision, and promised protection; in knowing Him—
Jesus Christ—as our Savior, Lord, and Teacher; in experiencing the
ministry of the Spirit, who is "the Comforter" (John 14:26 KJV);
and in learning that God keeps in perfect peace the person whose
mind is stayed on Him (Isaiah 26:3 ESV).

This is the Jesus-instructed teaching that awaits us in the pages
of *Consider the Lilies*. I can think of many reasons to commend it,
and just as many reasons to read it. One is that we have become a
society riddled with anxieties. The statistical indications are mind-
numbing in their indication of the vast numbers of people who take
prescription drugs for what is rarely a biologically caused problem.
The anxiety levels of young people have reached an all-time high.
If the numbers of those who contracted COVID-19 were of epidemic proportions, what can we say about the rising tide of anxiety
among the young? And, truth be told, there are reasons enough in
the Western world to flood human souls of every age with a deep-
seated anxiety. Is there no relief to be found outside of a medical
prescription?

Jonny Ardavanis is no stranger to these realities. He does not
write as an ivory-tower theoretician or a slick guru. During the years
of his pastoral ministry at camps, on a college campus, and in the
church, he has been in the trenches with multitudes of younger and
older people whose lives have been profoundly damaged by anxiety.
Nor has he had to seek anxiety-causing experiences in his own life;
they have come to him.

Jonny's experience, both personal and pastoral, has contributed
greatly to this book. It is, in many ways, the Maker's prescription manual. Jonny encourages us to seek the knowledge of God
Himself—Creator, Sustainer, Provider, Savior, and Lord. For only
in God Almighty will we experience deliverance from our deepest
fears and discover lasting peace.

As a wise and experienced spiritual physician, Jonny sees our anxiety, at its root, as a spiritual problem. Ultimately, therefore, its remedy must be theological. And because he is also a seasoned reader and expositor of Scripture, these pages are like an old-fashioned apothecary's shop whose shelves are stocked with wonderful medicines for the soul.

Consider the Lilies prods us to encounter the character of God, not in a merely theoretical way, but in the lives of tried and tested saints like Moses, Elijah, Job, and Paul. Its counsel is eminently practical. Each chapter concludes with diagnostic questions to guide us, and the medicine prescribed throughout the book has proven to bring healing to many down through the ages. The ultimate remedy for all our anxieties is to be found in God Himself. And Jonny shows us how we can discover His glorious and peace-giving character from His Word, and find rest in His Son Jesus Christ and in all that He has done for us and means to us.

So here is my recommendation: Whether you are struggling with anxiety or want to help someone who is, read these instructions, take the prescribed doses, and finish the course. You will feel better as a result.

Sinclair B. Ferguson,
CHANCELLOR'S PROFESSOR OF SYSTEMATIC THEOLOGY
AT REFORMED THEOLOGICAL SEMINARY;
TEACHING FELLOW AT LIGONIER MINISTRIES

Introduction

Welcome to *Consider the Lilies*. If you have picked up this book, odds are you or someone you love is worried or anxious.

I've been there too.

Truthfully, I never thought I would become a pastor. Nor did I ever anticipate writing a book—especially one related to worry and anxiety. In my ministry roles as a camp director, dean at a Christian university, and now as a pastor, I have seen the pain, angst, and confusion that plague the people of God. Worries howl in our minds like the winter wind, and the stresses and pressures of life make it difficult to tell where one worry stops and another one begins. College tuition? Car troubles? Heart problems? Rebellious child? The economy? I recently saw a T-shirt with these words boldly displayed across the front: "I've got 99 problems and anxiety is literally all of them." Maybe this is how you feel.

You may not be facing a tragedy right now, but deep down, you believe calamity and pain are coming your way and as a result you're anxious. If trouble has already struck, you assume it will surely strike again. You're longing for the internal clamor to stop. You're yearning for *peace*.

Providentially, I wrote this book during a difficult season of my life. I have battled my own health issues, but it was a different ball game to wait, pray, and pace the hospital corridors as we navigated significant medical challenges with our precious baby daughter. I write this book not as an occupant of the highbrow tower of expertise but as one who has come to experience the peace, joy, and comfort that our Father provides to His children in His Word and through His Spirit.

Not only have I had to navigate uncertainty, fear, and worry in my life, but I've walked through suffering with people whose pain far outweighs my own. At times I've wondered, *Am I qualified to speak to people who have walked through trials far darker than my own?* With that in mind, I find my burden to write is not because I may or may not have suffered on your level but because God through His Word offers hope and peace for the full range of human anxiety and worry.

As we look to the Bible and examine what God has to say about worry and anxiety, one powerful, comforting, and transforming truth emerges: *gazing at God's glorious character is the pathway to peace.*

When I use the word *anxiety* in this book, I am speaking of the state of mind in which we are filled with worry because we have set our minds on something less than the character of our good and loving God. Jesus says, "Do not be worried" (Matthew 6:25), he then goes on to illustrate that a misdirected gaze is at the heart of worry and anxiety. All too often, we focus on our problems, pressures, fears, and uncertainties, but Scripture says we must look to our heavenly Father and His loving and sovereign care for His creation.

Both our minds and bodies experience the effects of living as fallen creatures in a fallen world. Thus, I'm keen on appropriately addressing the reality that we are *holistic beings*. Martyn Lloyd-Jones wrote in *Spiritual Depression*, "You cannot isolate the spiritual from the physical for we are body, mind and spirit."[1] Thankfully, God's

Word speaks not only to the nourishment of our souls with clarity, gentleness, and wisdom but also to the stewardship and nourishment of our bodies.

Although not discussed in detail here, I believe there are times when we may need a skilled physician or competent biblical counselor to ascertain and address the various issues present in our bodies and souls. Moreover, there are indeed times when both our physical bodies and our spiritual souls overlap—they are integrated and interdependent in ways we cannot fully fathom.

My goal is simple: to help you behold the character of God. The Bible contains no secret sauce to peace; the answers to worry and anxiety are revealed in the plain reading of God's Word. The answer to anxiety has more to do with who God is than with who we are. The answer to our worry is not to look *inward* but to look *upward*. As we consider God's character, I urge you to pray and ask God's Holy Spirit to impress these truths upon your heart and, in turn, lead you to "the rock that is higher than I" (Psalm 61:2). In my own life, I have come to the settled conviction that the pursuit of God leads to intimacy with Him, intimacy leads to trust, trust produces peace, and peace leads to unassailable joy.

In the pages that follow, we will study the precious truth of the fatherhood of God. We will come to the great peaks of theology and behold His sovereignty, unfathomable love, comforting presence, and sufficient grace and power to those who trust in Him. Each chapter concludes with reflection questions based on the truths of Scripture we are examining. I pray these questions and the sections of God's Word provided will help you direct your gaze at God. After all, it's one thing to acknowledge and affirm God's attributes; it's an entirely different thing to behold, consider, and *gaze*.

I've titled this book *Consider the Lilies* because Jesus told His anxious followers to "consider the lilies" (Matthew 6:28 NKJV) so that they would more fully understand the power, care, and provision of God. My subtitle, *Finding Perfect Peace in the Character of God*, suggests that the peace of God does not fall into our laps as we sit and wait for it but rather is given by God to those who fix their minds *on* and fill their hearts *with* God's matchless and unchanging character.

In this light, peace is not so much something we find but rather something we receive as we gaze at God—which is the essence of faith. Logically, for us to know God's character, He must reveal Himself, and, amazingly, we find God's self-revelation in the Bible. God's Word, therefore, will not merely be the anecdotal sprinkling, but the main substance of this book and of the heart that comes to find true and lasting peace. This image—of the reception of God's peace because of our faith in the revelation of His character—is at the core of this book. *Everything* written here resides within that single teaching of Jesus.

In that spirit, here is my prayer for you as you begin this book:

> The steadfast of mind You will keep in perfect peace,
> Because he trusts in You.
> Trust in the LORD forever,
> For in GOD the LORD, we have an everlasting Rock.
>
> Isaiah 26:3–4

PART I

Our Fallen World

CHAPTER 1

Earth: A Painful and Confusing Place

I grew up a PK (a.k.a. "preacher's kid").

As a child, when people asked me, "Jonny, what do you want to do when you grow up?" I had one response: *play for the Los Angeles Lakers.* Unfortunately, I could hardly keep up with the guys at LA Fitness. Being five foot eleven (and a half) isn't necessarily conducive to becoming an NBA star. Even though other potential career fields floated around in my mind, there was one thing I knew with absolute certainty: *I don't want to be a pastor.*

In college I studied accounting and finance. My uncle Beebs (as we called him) told me accounting was "the language of business," so it seemed to be a good field of study for whatever I would go into *within* the business world. Looking back, I'm thankful I studied business, but I'm even more attuned to the truth that "the heart of man plans his way, but the LORD establishes his steps" (Proverbs 16:9 ESV).

Four years after graduating from college, I found myself in a new role—not in a financial firm or on the ground floor of a new start-up, but in Sequoia National Forest as a camp director. Although the Lord's shifting of my plans is a story for another time, I'm grateful that He moves His children not only through the opportunities He places before them but also through the burdens He places on their hearts. In God's timing, He leads us from *where we are* to *where He wants us to be.*

Each week of camp, one thousand teens, fresh off the sugar-high of the journey, would bolt out of their buses, and sauntering out behind them were their local church counselors and pastors who would be their weeklong cabinmates (a responsibility not for the faint of heart). Upon their arrival, a palpable euphoric high accompanied the opening moments of camp—the unloading of the luggage, the scurrying off to the cabins, and the dividing of campers into various teams for recreation. The whole scene was alive with life—an anthill of excitement for the week to come. My favorite view of these initial moments was from the elevated deck of Ponderosa Chapel. From this vantage point, I could see the beautiful lake, the Sequoia National Forest, and the picturesque mountains, and, amidst it all, I sensed all around me the buzz of commotion and anticipation for the week to come.

The students arrived on Sunday, and then, almost as quickly as they came, they departed on Saturday. They chattered among themselves as they climbed into the same buses that had brought them (although with much less energy and much more sugar than when they had come) and headed for home. Our staff would "flip camp" (as we say in camp language), and the next day (Sunday) another one thousand students would be bused in.

If there was a soundtrack behind the events taking place during those opening moments of camp, it would be "everything is awesome" (if you know, you know). However, the soundtrack of optimism, excitement, and joy would often be altered to a minor key by the first night of camp as I quickly became accustomed to the terms:

+ self-harm
+ panic attacks
+ suicidal thoughts
+ depression
+ anxiety

There was an obvious theme behind the smiles of the students who attended: they were anxious, fearful, or melancholy. So much so, that one article reads one-fourth of young adults in the past three years have considered the thought, *Should I take my life?*[1] According to psychologist Robert Leahy, "The average high school kid today has the same level of anxiety as the average psychiatric patient in the early 1950s."[2]

But it's not just teens who are anxious; it's adults as well. Anxiety affects and attacks people who are sixteen and sixty-three alike. Like a ski lift that never reaches the top of the mountain, the statistical rise of worry, fear, suicide, and depression never seems to plateau but only to aggressively escalate with time.

I'll never forget the way our camp nurses rushed to the aid of a teenage girl at camp who was convulsing and screaming as she clung to the leg of a chair. She gasped, "Help, I can't breathe!" We called for an ambulance, not knowing the extent of what was happening. Her younger sister came over and said, "She's having a panic attack. Just give her a few minutes." The sister sat down next to the seizing girl, rubbed her head, and patted her back. Moments later, the tears dried and the convulsing ceased. After gathering herself, the teenage girl looked at her younger sister and said, "At least it wasn't as bad as the episode I had yesterday."

These stories became one of the anthems of my experience. I rapidly realized that my responsibilities wouldn't just be fun and games but would include ministering to the multitude of teens crippled by fear, paralyzed by anxiety, and mangled by melancholy. It was as if the very souls of these students had been tied to an anchor and thrown into an endless sea of worry and fear. The root causes of their despair would differ—academic pressure, an abusive father, a mother who had died of cancer, trauma in their past, secret sin in their present, a breakup, financial difficulties, and so forth. I often asked students what was behind their anxiety, and their answers would range from "If I fail AP US History, I won't get into Stanford" to "I'm sixteen years old, and I've had three abortions. Will God ever forgive me?"

Regardless of the reasons for their anxiety, fear, or despair, I realized that people who are categorized as minors aren't dealing with *minor* problems at all, but rather *major* levels of anxiety and colossal degrees of depression.[3] At camp, I was interacting with students on a weekly basis who had contemplated or previously attempted suicide. On some occasions, our team had to life-flight students down the mountain because they had come to camp not to enjoy the week *but to end their lives.* Furthermore, the demographics of those afflicted by anxiety, fear, and melancholy included not only those who had grown up "rough" or in the foster-care system but also those growing up in the loving care of their parents and Sunday school teachers. Some teens are anxious because they grew up without parents; others are anxious because they are afraid of disappointing the loving ones they have.

The average teen today is growing up with more opportunities, possessions, and "friends" than ever, and yet they are lonelier and more anxious, panicked, and despairing than any generation that has preceded them.[4] Students are growing up in a world where they are better fed, connected, and educated than ever before, and yet they are the most medicated generation in human history.[5]

But again, it's not just young people. The largest consumers of antidepressants in America are not university students or high schoolers but women aged sixty and older. The National Center for Health Statistics reported that women sixty and older are twice as likely to take antidepressants as women eighteen to thirty-nine.[6] As I witnessed the broad scope of those who wrestle with anxiety and despair, I realized that if the pastors and counselors accompanying these students weren't battling worry or anxiety themselves, they were at least looking for biblical answers to equip them to minister to the people assigned to their care.

What Does God Say about My Anxious Heart?

During my second summer as a camp director, I began to host an optional seminar on the topic of fear and anxiety. I gave it the title "What Does the Bible Say about My Anxious Heart?" Although my seminar conflicted with the free-time activities of paddleboarding, paintball, and a variety of sports tournaments, students and counselors alike streamed into the chapel to hear what Jesus had to say about anxiety, fear, and depression. Two main questions seemed uppermost in the minds of the listeners: *Does God speak to my prevalent and persistent problem? And, if so, does He do so in a way that doesn't leave me feeling mainly condemned but rather provides me with the hope, comfort, and strength I need to trust Him?* I quickly discovered that people were not just afflicted by anxiety, but they were also disturbed by the guilt and shame that came from being anxious all the time. I taught iterations of this seminar for the next four years in various places, and over time my burden for the anxious and my love for God and His Word steadily grew.

New Roles, Same Problems

As was true for many people, my life changed during the season of COVID-19. After working as a camp director for five years, I took on a new role as the dean of campus life at The Master's University in Southern California. My focus was to oversee the thrice-weekly chapels, cultivate community, and minister to the twelve hundred students who attended. Unlike those who came to the evangelistic youth camp in the woods, these students were all professing believers. They attended Bible-preaching chapels, took theology classes, and lived in a campus community that sought to foster a love not only for Christ, but also for each other.

You may be thinking that the presence of anxiety would have been annihilated in this kind of environment. But similarly to the students I had encountered before, many of these university students were anxious about the future, fearful because of events in the past, and despairing because of circumstances in the present. Thoughts of self-harm or suicide were not foreign inside this scripturally staunch environment; they were simply better concealed.

No longer were these students temporary guests I interacted with for a week, but now residents of the campus community I had grown to love. It's not that they were disconnected from environments that proclaimed the truth of God's Word; rather, they were immersed in God's Word through their classes, the chapels they went to, and the churches they attended each Sunday. I found myself, once again, ministering to the melancholy and attending to the anxious.

Fast-forward to today. I now serve as the lead teaching pastor of Stonebridge Bible Church in Franklin, Tennessee. The individuals to whom I minister differ, the composition of their struggles vary, but the war that is waging on the battlefront of their minds is the same.

Is my job secure?
Are my children safe?
Will I ever get married?
Will I ever get pregnant?
Why did I have another miscarriage?

Will I be able to pay my mortgage?

Where is our country headed? Is World War III on the horizon?

Our lives are often a chronicle of trouble and pain—dashed hopes, miscarried babies, lost loved ones, relational heartbreak, stinging injustice, crippling illness, and chronic loneliness. Sometimes the pain we experience is like a flash flood that suddenly sweeps over our lives; at other times, our pain is like a slow leak that intensifies over time.[7] It's not only the catastrophic headlines of our lives that prompt our anxiety but also the details that fade into the background—a broken water heater, an impending job interview, years of prayers for a spouse, or thoughts of *Will I be single forever?* Fuel and food prices are soaring; an enemy nation is test-firing rockets into the ocean; and now I have a little mole on the back of my neck, causing me to wonder, *Is it cancerous?*

The National Alliance on Mental Illness claims that more than forty million adults in the United States have some form of anxiety disorder.[8] What's more, it is estimated that between $42 and $47 billion are spent annually on anxiety treatments and medications.[9] It's no wonder Kai Wright, a columnist for *The Nation,* started a popular podcast in 2016 titled *The United States of Anxiety.*[10] Our lives are inundated by the onslaught of relentless news and media coverage, and, as a result, we barely have time to process one crisis before another one is hurled in front of our eyes.

In a recent internet search, I typed in the words *cure for anxiety,* and 595 million results popped up in less than half a second.

I then proceeded to search the words *how can I find peace.* How many results do you think instantaneously populated? A staggering 1.54 billion.

Now, of course not all of those websites give an answer to my question. But the abundance of results illustrates my point perfectly. We are desperate for answers to our anxiety, and the "answers" offered by the world seem endless.

We live in an anxious world. All of us long for serenity and peace—yes, even the people of God. Contrary to the heretical conclusions of prosperity preachers today, God's children are not immune to suffering; instead, our pain is often more unexplainable, severe, and frequent than that of unbelievers.[11] Even now, as you take inventory of the trials, troubles, and worries of your life, you may be asking yourself, *Is there any hope?*

"A Strange, Mad, Painful Place"

I read J. I. Packer's classic book *Knowing God* when I was in college. As I read his opening chapter, I was struck by the rationality of worry and despair when God is removed from the picture. Packer wrote, "The world becomes a strange, mad, painful place, and life in it a disappointing and unpleasant business, for those who do not know about God. Disregard the study of God, and you sentence yourself to stumble and blunder through life blindfolded, as it were, with no sense of direction and no understanding of what surrounds you."[12]

Anxiety is only natural when we consider the reality of the world we live in—a world full of earthquakes, heartaches, divorce, and death. With that uncertainty, not to mention the grief and loss we know we can experience at any moment, doesn't anxiety make sense? What is truly *unnatural* is peace and trust. There is a reason Paul defined the peace that God gives as something that "surpasses all understanding" (Philippians 4:7 ESV). The world experiences peace *circumstantially*, but the Christian's peace is not anchored in happenstance or circumstance but in the character of our heavenly Father.

As this first chapter draws to an end, you, like the people of God throughout the centuries, may be asking yourself these two questions:

1. *How does God respond to my anxious heart?*
2. *What hope, peace, comfort, and joy does He offer me in His Word?*

We will take on these questions in the pages ahead, but for now just know that if you are living in perpetual anxiety, true and lasting peace will not, and cannot, be found in this world; it can come only from knowing God as He reveals Himself in His Word.

———— **Reflection Questions** ————

1. Write down some of the things you are anxious about. What might God be directing you to do in light of your anxieties?

2. What do you hope to glean from this book? In your experience of worry and anxiety, have you ever done a study on the character of God? How does your understanding of God's character apply to your everyday life?

3. If you are reading this book in a group study, name some ways you can pray for one another as you examine what God says about anxiety in His Word.

CHAPTER 2

Perfect Peace?

When I tell someone I'm from California, one of the most common questions they ask me is "Do you surf?"

My response: "No . . . not really."

Of course, I wish I could say yes. Who doesn't want to be a cool surfer, right? I did, however, work at a smoothie shack on Australia's Gold Coast, but that's another story for another time. To be honest, I'm somewhat intimidated by the ocean. Not just because of the sharks (of which there are seemingly millions), but because I possess a significant amount of respect for waves. Of course, there are times when the waves are nothing more than small speed bumps, but at other times the waves are like great towers that crush all that lies beneath. If you've been in the midst of an oceanic swell, you know what it's like to be pulverized by wave after wave as you hold your breath and fight toward the surface. These great breakers not only pummel the body but can discombobulate and dizzy the mind.

Powerful waves like these remind me of certain seasons of life. At times it may seem as though each new day brings another wave of adversity and disappointment. All our biographies possess a panoply of difficulty and trouble. Our minds are frequently disoriented and drenched by despair, and we often shrivel before the relentless tides of fear and uncertainty. Even as you read these words, anxiety may be lurking around every corner. One particular loitering fear may be robbing you of peace. What, then, is the initial foundation of hope and strength for our lives riddled by anxiety, despair, and melancholy? What can possibly buoy our souls amid the turbulent seas of this life?

Our Knowable Creator

In a world desperate for hope, the Bible provides the remedy our hearts are searching for: God's unchanging and matchless character is the antidote our worried and anxious souls need the most.

Remember our definition of anxiety? It's the inevitable worry, fear, and unrest that rises in our minds when we direct our gaze to the problems, pressures, and uncertainties of life rather than to God Himself. In most of life's seasons, we don't have a say about the pain or trouble we endure, nor the unknowns we face. We do, however, have a choice where we look—either at our worries or at God. People who behold the faithful character of God come to find that He, and He alone, is the one who calms the raging seas of our hearts. Even as the waves crash around us, God's character is constant and His power and love are sure.

In this chapter, I'll examine a biblical character who, though commended for his faithfulness, was lovingly corrected and mercifully strengthened by God in the moment of his fear, anxiety, and depression. You may be familiar with his story, but try to see it with fresh eyes as you ask yourself, *How does God respond to those who are anxious, fearful, and melancholy?*

Blameless Job in a Pile of Ashes

What does it mean to be blameless? It's hard to imagine in a fallen world, isn't it? The Hebrew word *tam* is used fifteen times in the Old Testament. The word means "blameless," "guiltless," "without fault." Of the fifteen times, only *once* does it refer to a human being—Job. Job was a wealthy, respected, and *blameless* man who feared the Lord and turned away from evil (Job 1:1, 8). This was not your average guy who believed in a higher deity. Job was a devout, faithful, and committed servant of Yahweh. But the blissful introduction to Job's life cinematically shifts when the narrator of the book transports us to a conversation that took place between God and Satan.

Satan suggested that Job was blameless and righteous only because God had richly blessed him. Therefore Satan proposed that God allow him to take everything away from Job, and then, finally, Job would curse God. God granted permission, and, in a matter of verses, Job's life was torn apart. First a messenger came and said that Job's servants had been slaughtered (Job 1:15). Another messenger told Job that his sheep and servants were consumed by a fire from heaven (1:16), and then a third messenger reported that the "Chaldeans formed three units and made a raid on the camels and took them, and slew the servants with the edge of the sword" (1:17).

These successive reports were like daggers to Job's heart, but the most painful report was yet to come: "Another also came and said, 'Your sons and your daughters were eating and drinking wine in their oldest brother's house, and behold, a great wind came from across the wilderness and struck the four corners of the house, and it fell on the young people and they died, and I alone have escaped to tell you'" (Job 1:18–19).

How would you have responded? Can you imagine that degree of shock, pain, and grief?

Tragically, some of you don't have to stretch your imaginations very far. I recently talked with a woman who had suffered the loss of, not one, but two children. Our world is broken, and our hearts have likewise been broken by the anguish of loss.

How did Job respond?

> Then Job arose and tore his robe and shaved his head, and he fell to the ground and worshiped. He said,
>
> > "Naked I came from my mother's womb,
> > And naked I shall return there.
> > The LORD gave and the LORD has taken away.
> > Blessed be the name of the LORD."
>
> Through all this Job did not sin nor did he blame God. (Job 1:20–22)

Stunningly, Job's reaction to calamity was praise.

But Satan wasn't finished. After another conversation with God, "Satan went out from the presence of the LORD and smote Job with sore boils from the sole of his foot to the crown of his head. And he took a potsherd to scrape himself while he was sitting among the ashes" (Job 2:7–8). The chapter ends with these words: "His pain was very great" (v. 13). What an understatement! His children were dead; his servants were dead; his cattle and livestock were dead; his house had been destroyed. And now he was sitting in the dirt, scratching his boils with a shard of pottery as his wife urged him to "curse God and die!" (v. 9).

Despite these difficult circumstances, "Job did not sin" (Job 2:10). But the book of Job is longer than two chapters. In fact, it's forty-two chapters, and by the middle of the book, the afflicted man who had initially said "Blessed be the name of the LORD" (1:21) was crying out with a profound level of anxiety and despair:

"And now my soul is poured out within me;
        days of affliction have taken hold of me."

Job 30:16 ESV

"God has cast me into the mire,
        and I have become like dust and ashes.
I cry to you for help and you do not answer me;
        I stand, and you only look at me."

Job 30:19–20 ESV

"My inward parts are in turmoil and never still;
        days of affliction come to meet me.
I go about darkened, but not by the sun;
        I stand up in the assembly and cry for help.
I am a brother of jackals
        and a companion of ostriches.
My skin turns black and falls from me,
        and my bones burn with heat.
My lyre is turned to mourning,
        and my pipe to the voice of those who weep."

Job 30:27–31 ESV

The severity of Job's suffering prompted the tune of his life to be that of mourning and weeping. The life had been sucked out of him. Like a popped balloon, Job was free-falling into a pit of crippling anxiety and depression. Can you blame him? Job said his "inward parts are in turmoil and never still" (Job 30:27 ESV), meaning that the most fitting word to describe his life was *gutted*. Assuredly all of us have gone through something difficult, if not heartbreaking, but when we consider the extent of Job's suffering, we are compelled to wonder, *How does God respond to the anxiety-ridden in circumstances like these?*

The Whirlwind

God's response to Job's profound despair is indicative of the way He responds to all His anxious, fearful, and despairing creatures in the Bible. His reply is not based on circumstances, nor does He explain His providential plan to those who ask for answers. He routinely responds in one way: *He proclaims His own character.*

God doesn't say, "Let Me tell you why this is happening." He says, "Let Me tell you who I am."

The strongest remedy, the surest balm, and the most comforting pillow God provides for the despairing and anxious is the revelation of His own nature. God initially asked Job probing questions, not because He was searching for answers, but because He routinely prompts His anxious, depressed, and fearful children to *think.* One of the chief aspects of God's image bearers is that we have a mind, and God wants those who are anxious to use it.

To a man whose life had been shackled to sorrow, God responded by asking him questions that compelled him to consider the character of the God he had started to question:

+ Where were you when I laid the earth's foundation? (Job 38:4).
+ Do you tell the waves, "This is how far you may come and no farther"? (38:11).
+ Have you ever commanded the morning? (38:12).
+ Do you summon the rain? (38:25, 28).
+ Do you bind the chains of the stars? (38:31).
+ Does the lightning report to you and ask you where to strike? (38:35).
+ Is it by your understanding that birds soar? (39:26).
+ Have you ever given anything to God—the One to whom

everything under heaven belongs—that would compel Him
to repay you? (41:11).

God continued this line of questioning for nearly four chapters (Job 38–41). And at the conclusion of God's questioning, Job
said, "I have heard of You by the hearing of the ear; but now my
eye sees You; therefore I retract, and I repent in dust and ashes"
(Job 42:5–6). Job understood that his own worry and despair
were rooted in a deficient understanding of God's character. Job's
anxiety and despair may have seemed reasonable in light of the
circumstances, but in view of God's character and questions, Job
said "I repent."

It's precious to me that, at the end of the book that bears his
name, James said it was these questions that compelled Job to
consider the compassion and mercy of God (James 5:11). To His
anxious servant Job, God displayed not only His wisdom and sovereignty but also His tender and abundant mercy. Job had summoned
God to the court of his own sense of justice. Job's experience had
been truly traumatic—there is no denying or downplaying the pain
that marked his life! Everything he possessed and nearly everyone
he loved had been killed, stolen, burned, or destroyed. Yet despite
all of these realities, God never gave Job any explanation for all his
suffering and pain. He never told Job about the conversation that
took place between Him and Satan. At the end of the book, God
vindicated Job, but before He did so, He painted a canvas with vivid
colors that illustrated who He is.

Have you ever realized that your every worry is an invitation
to draw closer to God? That every anxiety in your life compels you
to direct your gaze to someplace or someone? One of the primary
purposes of trials in our lives is to wean us from this world and strip
us of earthly hope so that we would cling to the hope and strength
that can only come from God (James 1:2–4). Remarkably, for those

who set their minds and fix their gaze on God, He provides His children with what our hearts are searching for—peace. God did not remove Job's problems, but He does, for those who draw near to Him, provide a supernatural peace even amidst unfathomable pain and relentless uncertainty.

The Revelation of God

Our understanding of God's character constitutes either the cause or the cure of our anxiety. For example, whenever I doubt God's provision, I am worried about all my needs. When I doubt His control, I worry about all the perceived chaos. When I doubt His love, I foolishly live as if I could do anything to deserve His love (which leads to anxiety because of my constant failures and sin). But as we have just examined (and may have taken for granted), for us to know God's character, He must reveal Himself. Thankfully, we have a God who is there, and as Francis Schaeffer once said, "He is not silent." God speaks to us in the Bible. Of course, you may already affirm that, but it's likely a good reminder for you who may have picked up this book searching for an answer for your anxiety. Because truly, everything true and comforting in my book owes its origin to what is within God's Word.

In God's Word we come to know Him and what He is like, not exhaustively, but intimately. Maybe you already know and believe that God is "lofty and exalted" (Isaiah 6:1), but have you come to the realization that He is not aloof? Maybe you have come to know that He is, in fact, divine (Isaiah 46:9), but have you realized He is not distant (Psalm 46:7)? Do you think God is far off? The Bible says He is very findable. He is personal. He understands your pain, and He is "a very present help in trouble" (Psalm 46:1 ESV). As Charles Spurgeon (1834–1892) noted, "You are not the first child of God" to be despairing and anxious,[1] nor will you be the last, but the God who is Himself "the First and the Last" (Revelation 1:8 NLV) brings His truth to bear on our anxious hearts as we set our gaze on Him.

If you are familiar with the Bible, you may read the accounts of faithful men and women and wonder, *Do they ever falter like I do?* Thankfully, the scriptural biographies of the most blameless, bold, and faithful also possess the transparent inclusion of their lapses in trust and departures from joy. The Bible presses us toward a high standard of godliness, but it also necessarily includes the knots and wrinkles of its godliest characters. There are no perfect characters in the story God is writing, only a perfect God.

Have you ever asked:

"God, where are you?"
"Why have you abandoned me?"

Or even said, "What's the point? Life itself is but a slow death . . ."? If so, you find yourself seated at a great table of saints in Scripture whose circumstances may differ from yours but whose struggle is the same. Our questions and sorrows find their voice in the stories we read in the Bible. Their lives *then* and our lives *now* were not and are not a series of endless triumphs. Our lives are often full of tragedy, trouble, heartache, and pain. The Bible's central characters are not emotionless giants that dispel all fear around them, nor are they immune to anxiety and despair, but, on the contrary, they are in constant need of grace and strength from God.

What Comes to Your Mind?

In his book *The Knowledge of the Holy*, A. W. Tozer penned the well-remembered line: "What comes into our minds when we think about God is the most important thing about us."[2] Indeed, this is true! Furthermore, what comes into your mind when you think about God is the surest weapon, comfort, and encouragement you have in your battle against anxiety and despair. In both the Old and New Testaments, God responded to those who were anxious by mounting the divine pulpit and preaching a sermon on His own character. *Who He is, is the antidote to our worries and fears.* Jesus used the phrase "O ye of little faith" four times in the Gospels (Matthew 6:30; 8:26; 16:8; Luke 12:28 KJV), and He always employed this phrase in the context of the disciples' worry and fear. In such instances, Jesus reminded His disciples of His powerful, providential, and loving character. Jesus did not simply tell His followers to snap out of it or cut it out! He was firm in His rebuke, yet loving and tender in providing the abundant reasoning for our trust in Him. He Himself "knows our frame; He is mindful that we are but dust" (Psalm 103:14). We are not oaks; we are reeds. And not whole reeds at that; we are "bruised" (Matthew 12:20 NIV). The bravest of people are all damaged, bent, and frail. And what the *bruised* need is someone who is strong, someone who is mighty, and someone who "cares for you" (1 Peter 5:7 NIV). God's care, however, although an objective reality, is experienced only in a practical and subjective sense by those who plant their lives deeply in the soil of God's Word. I remember praying for a deeper conviction of God's care, then realizing that the answer to my prayer lay right in front of me on my desk: my consistent and persistent exposure to God's Word is the catalyst to the cemented conviction of His care. For years I believed I had a flawed understanding of faith. I thought my faith was something I "placed" in Jesus Christ *once upon a time.* That may be true with regard to salvation, but, in the Bible, faith is not merely an affirmation of truth; it is a constant *exercise*—faith is not a *thing*; it is an *action.*

God's response to Job is emblematic of the way He responds to all His despairing servants throughout the Bible. You may wonder: *How does Jesus respond to the anxious?* Well, since our God does not change, neither does the prescription provided.

In His most famous sermon, the Sermon on the Mount, Jesus addressed people like us—worried, fearful, and despairing. Jesus exposed the prominent causes of anxiety and fear and then provided a prohibition: "Do not be anxious" (Matthew 6:25 ESV). Thankfully, He did not stop there. Jesus then bade His anxious followers to dwell deeply on the character of God. He didn't merely prompt them to nod in agreement regarding the truths He proclaimed but rather summoned them to activate their minds, anchor their hopes, and fixate their gazes on the character of their heavenly Father. Jesus beckoned the anxious to "look at the birds" (Matthew 6:26) and "consider the lilies" (Matthew 6:28 NKJV) because if our heavenly Father cares for them, how much more will He care, love, and provide for those who are made in His image? Jesus said that when we are anxious about the things of the world, we are living just like the Gentiles (Matthew 6:32)—those who didn't know God. Meaning that to be a worried Christian is a contradiction of terms because it fails to reckon who we have as our heavenly Father.

If you're a Christian, life is assuredly full of suffering, sorrow, and pain—and yet we read: "Trust in the LORD with all your heart" (Proverbs 3:5). How can this be? At times this command seems impossible. But it must be understood that trusting God is possible only if we know what He is like and saturate our minds with the truth of why we should trust Him. Faith is not a blind jump, it's a reasoned response to the truth of who God is. The more we pursue this lofty endeavor of knowing God and beholding His character, the more we can affirm the words of Isaiah with which we began:

You keep him in perfect peace
    whose mind is stayed on you,
    because he trusts in you.

Isaiah 26:3 ESV

—————— Reflection Questions ——————

1. How would it change your life if you fully realized that every anxiety is an invitation to draw closer to God? What are some worries you are facing right now that could be an invitation to draw nearer to your heavenly Father?

2. Why does God respond to the anxious with a proclamation of His character? What does that tell us about worry?

3. God doesn't promise an easy life, but He does provide a supernatural peace to those who trust in Him. Read Isaiah 26:3—what is the prerequisite to experiencing the perfect peace of God? What does it mean to "stay" our minds on God?

CHAPTER 3

Embodied Beings

Remember how I told you I wanted to play professional basketball? Of course, I barely played on my high school team, but a young hooper can dream, can't he? God made it clear that wasn't His plan in two ways:

1. I wasn't good enough (He can't get any clearer than that).
2. Every time I play, I dislocate my shoulder.

One time while I was playing basketball with several missionary kids in Papua New Guinea, a student ran through my outstretched arm, badly breaking and tearing the bones and ligaments in my shoulder. The year before, I had undergone an operation on the same shoulder, but this injury was different. For the remainder of the trip, I kept my arm in a makeshift sling, and when I got home, the doctors told me that my labrum, rotator cuff, and bicep tendon were torn, but not only that—I had also endured significant axillary nerve damage.

For almost two years I could not and did not move my arm at all. In fact, the surgeons told me I may never move that arm again. As a guy that was very used to exercise and recreation and had just nursed the same arm back to full strength, I found that this season was one in which I not only faced physical challenges but also walked through profound discouragement and frustration in my mind and heart. Injuries can be debilitating. In the few years leading up to that injury, I had broken both knees, torn both shoulders, and undergone various surgical operations. And even though my injuries may pale in comparison to the injuries of others, I found it to be true that our physical bodies have the ability to influence our minds. Whether it be fatigue, hunger, pain, sleeplessness, or sickness, we see in our own lives and in the lives of those in the Bible that there are natural and physical factors that contribute to anxiety, fear, and despair.

A. W. Tozer once said that "nothing less than a whole Bible can make a whole Christian."[1] Tozer's point was that no one passage of Scripture provides a comprehensive framework for any matter or any topic. Again, we need the *whole* Bible to make a *whole* Christian. And in Scripture we see that it would be extreme to say that the underlying recipe of *all* anxiety and depression is *always spiritual*, and it would also be extreme to say that the root cause of *all* anxiety is *always physical*. (Although I believe anxiety and despair are far more spiritual than they are physical.) Today in church culture, there is often an aggressive swing of the pendulum from one side to the other, but in Scripture and in church history, there are examples of both. Scripture is sufficient (2 Timothy 3:16), which means that everything we need "pertaining to life and godliness" is found in God's Word (2 Peter 1:3). And in the Bible, God clearly addresses the reality that we are *body, soul, and mind*. We are embodied beings. As Martyn Lloyd-Jones once articulated, we cannot demarcate our *spiritual* lives from our *physical* lives.

God's People Get Anxious and Depressed

In Mark's Gospel, Jesus, whose glory had been veiled during His incarnation (Philippians 2:5–6), revealed Himself to Peter, James, and John in an unparalleled manner. Jesus' glory was marvelously manifested as He was transfigured before them. Mark 9:3 records, "His garments became radiant and exceedingly white, as no launderer on earth can whiten them." Not only was His glory vibrantly displayed, but "Elijah appeared to them along with Moses; and they were talking with Jesus" (Mark 9:4). No man can see the full orbed glory of God and live, and yet, here, in this gracious condescension, Jesus displayed His radiance, and the crescendo of this scene was when the voice of the Father declared from heaven: "This is My beloved Son; listen to Him!" (Mark 9:7). John and Peter would later highlight this experience throughout their epistles by articulating that they were "eyewitnesses of His majesty" (2 Peter 1:16). Not only were they eyewitnesses of Christ's majesty, but they were also witnesses of two Old Testament legends: Moses and Elijah.

Moses was the greatest leader in the Old Testament. The heart of his story began not when he was a young man but when he was eighty years old. He was commissioned by God to deliver the Israelites from their Egyptian bondage (Exodus 3–4). He spoke to God "face to face" (Exodus 33:11) and relayed God's Word to God's people as the author of the Law (Genesis–Deuteronomy).

Moses was the lawgiver, but alongside Jesus on the Mount of Transfiguration was the Law's greatest guardian and most faithful witness—Elijah. This beacon of faithfulness, whose name means "God is my strength," was the greatest of the Old Testament prophets and appeared on the scene of Israelite history during a time of profound spiritual darkness and moral declension. Prior to Elijah's call as the prophet of God, the most ubiquitous description of the kings of Israel was that they did "evil in the sight of the Lord"

(1 Kings 15:26, 34; 16:19, 25, 30). As was the case with many of the prophets, Elijah's ministry began abruptly . . . and powerfully.

- Elijah *prayed* and for three years not a single drop fell from the sky (1 Kings 17:1).
- Elijah *prayed* and the widow's son rose from the dead (1 Kings 17:21–22).
- Elijah *prayed* and called down fire from heaven in his epic duel with the false prophets of Baal (1 Kings 18:36–38).
- Elijah *prayed* and rain fell from the sky after the three-and-a-half-year drought (1 Kings 18:42).

While examining the ministries of both Moses and Elijah, we must also consider that there were only two great eras of miracles in all the Old Testament. When? During the time of Moses's and Elijah's ministries. Miracles were not random occurrences in Scripture; they were performed at strategic points to validate the message and mission God had given to specific individuals. These miracles (the plagues; the division of the Red Sea; extraordinary drought, rain, fire, and so on) performed through Yahweh's power were the evidence that Moses and Elijah acted and spoke on behalf of the one true God. Bottom line: Moses and Elijah are the top-tier heroes of the Old Testament. They are the premier examples of faithfulness, boldness, and courage.

Thankfully, the Bible includes not only the triumphs and heroics of its most prominent characters but also their human weaknesses, lapses in trust, and departures from joy. Abraham lied, David committed murder and adultery, Noah got drunk, Peter denied Christ, and even the most stalwart of God's people (such as Moses and Elijah) have been bludgeoned by doubt and badgered by anxiety and despair. I say this not to justify any ungodly worry, but simply to say that even those who are known as "pillars of the faith" are only as strong as the God who sustains them. In examining their stories briefly, I want to consider some of the physical factors that may lead to anxiety and depression, even among the noblest of men.

Temperament

When Jesus saves a sinner, He gives them a new heart with new desires (Ezekiel 36:26), but regeneration of the heart doesn't necessarily mean renewal of the natural temperament. This means that there are some people who, by natural disposition, are more introspective and prone to despair and others who are more extroverted and susceptible to superficiality. We are all called into one family in Christ, but no child of God is the same. We are all in the same fight, but every child of God faces a different battle. Martyn Lloyd-Jones in his classic work *Spiritual Depression* stated: "There is nothing more futile . . . than to act on the assumption that all Christians are identical in every respect."[2] Every individual is made in the image of God, but every individual has a distinct temperamental and constitutional framework. Therefore, in dealing with the subject of anxiety or depression, it is important, in the words of Lloyd-Jones, that we begin by "understanding ourselves."[3] We each have various strengths, weaknesses, and natural dispositions, and biblical wisdom entails that we know our weaknesses and, ultimately, know ourselves. Natural temperament never is an excuse for ungodly worry, but understanding our own disposition helps us understand our vulnerabilities and susceptibilities with regard to anxiety and despair.

Elijah, the prayer warrior, miracle performer, and bulwark of boldness, will at one point, immediately following his epic duel with the false prophets of Baal, become so depressed that he begs God to take his life (1 Kings 19:4). How could a man experience such high degrees of spiritual triumph and then moments later be in the doldrums of depression and pray for death? We will examine a few different causes, but initially we must consider Elijah's natural temperament. James 5:17 details that "Elijah was a man like us" (NCB). I believe that when the half brother of our Lord noted the similarity between Elijah and the common man, he referred not only to the impact of his prayer but also to the monumental lows he experienced in his despair because of his natural temperament.

The best of men in Scripture are men at best. They aren't superheroes. They are at times men who are profoundly weak and in dire need of strength and encouragement from a powerful God. If you find yourself among those with the natural temperament of introspection, this isn't cause for further despair, considering that many of those whom God used in monumental ways belonged to the introspective and temperamental category. Again, this does not excuse a sinful lack of joy, nor an ungodly worry, but it draws our attention to the diversity of personalities and propensities that are represented in Scripture. Jeremiah, John the Baptist, Paul, Luther, Bunyan, and a great host of other men and women faced the same temptation to despair and worry and yet were still mightily used by God.

Physical Infirmity

You cannot isolate the spiritual from the physical for we are body, mind and spirit.

MARTYN LLOYD-JONES[4]

After God commissioned Moses to deliver His people, Moses responded by asking God to "send someone else" (Exodus 4:13 ESV). Why? Because of Moses's "faltering lips" (Exodus 6:12 NIV). Scripture details that the greatest lawgiver and leader of Israel experienced anxiety for an interesting reason: he stuttered. Moses wasn't a fluid orator with a booming voice; he was a stutterer commissioned by Yahweh to be the general, prophet, and pastor of two million people. Moses's physical inability contributed to his doubt, insecurity, and social anxiety: "I have never been eloquent" (Exodus 4:10).

In that same vein, Charles Spurgeon, the pastor at the Metropolitan Tabernacle in London and the minister recognized as the "Prince of Preachers," is well-known not only for his penetrating insight and powerful exposition but also for his well-chronicled battle with depression. Spurgeon himself stated plainly: "I find myself frequently depressed—perhaps more so than any other person here."[5] The predominant explanation Spurgeon would often provide for his depression was the fact that he suffered from gout. This gouty condition caused consistent pain throughout Spurgeon's body, and for the second half of his life, he would be forced to suspend himself from his ministerial duties because of his agonizing pain and badgering illnesses. From 1871 to the end of his life in 1892, Spurgeon hardly ever experienced a time when he wasn't undergoing some form of physical suffering. This pain prompted sleeplessness, and the great preacher would remark at one point, "It is a great mercy to get one hour's sleep at night."[6]

Although physical ailment and temperamental disposition are not distantly related, they are worth distinguishing. Often, however, the former does lead to the latter. Physical infirmity can lead to such profound levels of discouragement that it may seem as if we have the birthmark of sadness upon our souls. A stuttering mouth that prompts social anxiety, gout that prompts pain, or a thyroid irregularity that results in improper functionality of the chemicals in our body—our bodies are not divorced from our minds and souls. Nay, they are wedded together. Conversely, as we will soon observe, spiritual rebellion and persistent sin (as in David's adultery) can lead to deep and profound physical pain. David said, "When I kept silent about my sin, my body wasted away" (Psalm 32:3).

Exhaustion

Prior to his prayer for death, Elijah experienced total burnout. At Mount Carmel, Elijah had experienced a great spiritual victory (1 Kings 18:36–40). He had called down fire from heaven, defeated the false prophets of Baal, and then once again prayed that God would send rain—and, for the first time in three and a half years, God did (v. 45). This euphoric high was followed by his fifteen- to twenty-mile run from Carmel to Jezreel—so fast did Elijah run that he beat King Ahab's chariot (v. 46)! Upon his arrival in Jezreel, Elijah expected a kingdom revival. *Surely now the people will realize that Yahweh, and Yahweh alone, is God.* Elijah anticipated repentance from King Ahab and especially from the wicked Queen Jezebel. But Elijah's expectation of national repentance shattered when he was told that Queen Jezebel, rather than being repentant, was resolved to kill him (19:2).

The exhaustion that comes from a twenty-mile sprint, the inevitable hunger that follows a three-year drought, and the sleeplessness that came from fleeing for his life may all seem like secondary observations, but God graciously includes these details in His Word. This mighty man whose name means "God is my strength" becomes as weak as water when faith in God was not a constant exercise and when his energy had evaporated. Of course, fatigue is never an excuse for disobedience, but those who possess exhausted bodies and sapped minds are especially vulnerable to anxiety and despair. God's image bearers are not made from steel, they are made from the dust. We are men, not machines. Therefore, the aftermath of prolonged sleeplessness, hunger, and burnout is often anxiety and despair. Thankfully, God is mindful of our frame, and He knows that we are dust (Psalm 103:14). To His despairing servant Elijah, God not only proclaimed His character, but He also gave Elijah a nap and a snack. Before God strengthened Elijah's soul with the truth of His character, He strengthened and nourished his weary body.

Loneliness

Repeatedly throughout the opening pages of Genesis we read that God observed His creation and declared what He saw to be "good." In Genesis 2, however, we read that something was not good: "It is not good for the man to be alone" (Genesis 2:18). Of course, the thrust of this passage is God's fashioning of the woman for the man, but the principle remains true: God's image bearers were not intended to be creatures of isolation; they were made to dwell with their Creator and with *each other.*

Elijah's despair came on the heels of a three-and-a-half-year period when his only company was that of a widow and her son. This lack of community and deprivation of fellowship are not ancillary symptoms, but some of the underlying contributions. Part of being made in God's image means that we were made for relationships, and when life is starved of them, fear and melancholy inevitably follow. Ironically, we live in a world where we are more connected to more people than at any other time in history, yet we have never felt more alone. The technology we employ that is supposed to connect us with one another has functioned as a catalyst for our profound sense of disconnection. Life was meant to be lived together. It's not wrong to be an introvert (I think I might be becoming one), but it's spiritually sapping, soul sucking, and depressing to be subject to prolonged periods of loneliness.

Trauma

I am no stranger to horrifying stories that prompt despair and anxiety. Often these memories are so deeply embedded within our minds that we seem to relive these traumatic experiences every day. The moment we feel as if these horrific memories have faded, the fear begins to rise in our hearts as we consider the possibility that these memories are not just past experiences but future possibilities once more. For years in camping ministry, I think because I was removed from the immediate context of the campers' personal lives, I was viewed as a "safe space" for them to divulge the horrifying and traumatic evil they had endured. I was often told, and then obligated to document and report, heartbreaking and tear-jerking stories that I could scarcely bear to repeat. I was already convinced of the evil in the world, but few things solidified that conviction like the stories I heard in camping ministry over the years. In cases that involved an abusive relationship, sexual abuse, violence, and so forth, I would encourage the individual to meet with a skilled and experienced biblical counselor.

Furthermore, in some cases, such as postpartum depression, the individual may benefit from both a godly biblical counselor and a skilled physician who can help to regulate the abnormalities taking place. As mentioned before, we are not only souls—we are also bodies.

We will soon observe in greater detail how God responded to the traumatic experiences of Job (whose entire family died), King David (who ran for his life for more than a decade), and Elijah (whose fellow prophets had been murdered by Queen Jezebel). For now, we find comfort in the promise that God's goodness is so pervasive that it has the power to redeem even the darkest and evilest moments of life, and His grace is deeper than any evil or affliction.

Grief

The believer is no stranger to sorrow. The Christian life is not one mountain peak after another but is often lived in "the valley of the shadow of death" (Psalm 23:4). Paul wrote that the Christian is "sorrowful yet always rejoicing" (2 Corinthians 6:10). We live in a fallen world and our lives are often full of disappointment, pain, and unbearable grief—the lost loved one, the miscarried child, abandonment, betrayal, and so on. Grief is not wrong. Prolonged seasons of grief are not wrong. But when grief gives way to despair and is divorced from a proper mooring to the hope we have in Christ, despair becomes depression. In some cases, the attributes of God that are supposed to comfort us (such as God's sovereignty) thrust us deeper into the miry bog of grief when not necessarily tethered to His love and wisdom.

Digging Up Roots

The lonely, exhausted, melancholy, grieving, and disabled are loved by God. Their physical conditions, temperaments, situations, and pasts might make them more vulnerable to anxiety, but they are never excused from the worry that comes from unbelief. Interestingly, the audience Jesus addresses were no foreigners to trauma. They were ruled by the Roman Empire, which was known for raping women and crucifying their enemies. Fear and trauma were not unknown possibilities; they were everyday realities. Yet, despite these realities, Jesus told his followers, "Do not be worried about your life" (Matthew 6:25).

In mentioning the subjects of grief, infirmity, sickness, exhaustion, and trauma, I recognize that I do not know your personal story. Thankfully, the God who will one day make "all things new"

(Revelation 21:5) tells us He is, in the meantime, "the God of all comfort, who comforts us in all our troubles" (2 Corinthians 1:3–4 NIV). What a balm for our souls amid any sort of affliction and pain! Our God is not only the God of the whole universe; He is also "the God of all comfort." In this life we may mourn, but Jesus says to you through His Word, "Blessed are those who mourn, for they will be comforted" (Matthew 5:4 NIV). Maybe you have come to Jesus for the forgiveness of sins, but have you come to Him as the only source of comfort in this life? If not, Jesus bids you to come.

What happens in our bodies, to our bodies, and with our bodies cannot be separated from what is happening in our hearts. We are "fearfully and wonderfully made" (Psalm 139:14 NIV). We are woven together by God, and the Bible speaks with clarity to the intricacy and interdependence of our bodies and minds.

Reflection Questions

1. How did God display His kindness and mindfulness to anxious Elijah? What does that tell us about God? What does that tell us about God's image bearers?

2. Take stock of your physical well-being. Is there anything you can do to care for your body to support a healthy mind and spirit? The basics are good work—rest, good food, exercise, play, and so forth.

3. How did loneliness contribute to Elijah's despair? As God's image bearers, we have been created for relationship with God and with others. How can the presence of faithful people help in your battle against worry and anxiety? How can you seek to further embrace the relational way God has made you?

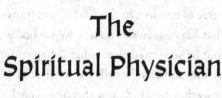

CHAPTER 4

The Spiritual Physician

My parents had seven children in nine years. Apparently, they really latched on to Psalm 127:4–5: "Like arrows in the hand of a warrior, so are the children of one's youth. Blessed is the man whose quiver is full of them." I'm the third of the seven. The order goes as follows: girl, boy, boy, girl, girl, girl, girl—so two boys, five girls. After the fifth baby, my dad told us that my mom was pregnant with twins—*surely one of them was going to be a boy!* No—out came Lindsey and Lauren. I'm tremendously grateful now, but upon realization the boys would be outnumbered forever, we did what any other boys would do—we cried.

My brother, Kyle, is an orthopedic surgeon. We have the same mother but apparently do not possess the same mental or hand-eye coordination (I'm taller by a couple of inches, so I've got him there). Throughout our lives, my brother has conducted many surgeries, and, ironically, I've undergone many surgeries. I do not know *how* he does his job, but I have experienced firsthand the type of operations he performs. By the time of surgery, the patient has typically already been to various appointments, undergone MRIs and X-rays, and performed physical therapy exercises to reduce inflammation. Good surgeons, like all good physicians, do not simply operate or prescribe medication, nor do they merely address the symptoms, but rather they conduct a careful consideration of the underlying causes and corresponding symptoms before extending the remedy.

The Good Physician

In Matthew 6, we find ourselves at a scene on the Mount of Beatitudes. Here, on this hillside overlooking the northern shore of the Sea of Galilee, history's most well-known sermon was delivered by history's most well-known preacher. Here we read Jesus' magnum opus on life in the kingdom of God, and in His sermon Jesus was focusing on one main thing—the relationship the Christian has with God as their heavenly Father.

Jesus' followers were anxious and fearful. They were under an oppressive Roman regime that was known for its violence and ruthless cruelty. You may remember it was Herod Antipas, the tetrarch of Galilee, who chopped off the head of John the Baptist—the greatest Jewish man who ever lived other than Jesus Christ (Matthew 11:11). We might believe that ancient fears are different from our own, but the followers of Christ *then* possessed many of the same worries and fears we face *now*: *Will I be able to provide for my family? Am I safe? Will God meet my needs? What about my loved ones' needs?* In Matthew 6:25, Jesus addressed the issue of anxiety by saying, "Therefore I tell you, *do not be anxious about your life*, what you will eat or what you will drink, nor about your body, what you will put on. Is not life more than food, and the body more than clothing?" (ESV, emphasis added).

One more time.

Jesus said, "Do not be anxious."

Maybe you suppress these words because they cause you to swell up with shame. But remember, Jesus is loving in His rebuke, and He is compassionate in providing not only the prohibition but the reasoning and power for why and how we can find peace.

Now, before we proceed, we need to examine this question: *What is the anxiety Jesus is referring to?*

Merimnao: Care? Concern? Or Anxiety?

In the New Testament, the Greek word *merimnao* is translated a few different ways—the first two being "care" and "concern," and the third being "anxiety" or "worry."

Perhaps you've heard the phrase "It's just semantics," and maybe that's what comes to mind when you see the words *care, concern,* and *anxiety.* Personally, I've never liked the phrase, because words aren't "just semantics"; they are everything. Specificity of definition matters as it relates to any subject in the Bible— especially as it relates to the subject of anxiety and worry and the character of God. Before continuing in our examination of Jesus' teaching about anxiety, it is critical that we firmly grasp a thorough understanding of the definition of anxiety and know how to biblically distinguish legitimate care and concern from ungodly worry and anxiety.

Concern

The apostle Paul loved the Philippian church; he had spent time there during his second missionary journey. As Paul reflected on his time with the Philippian church, he thanked God and expressed his longing to be with them with the affection of Christ Jesus (Philippians 1:3, 8). Paul, however, could not be united with the church he cared deeply about. Why? Because he was in a Roman prison when he wrote his letter to the Philippian church (vv. 7, 13, 17). But because he was concerned for their spiritual progress and desired to remind them of their citizenship in heaven, Paul detailed that he would be sending Timothy to them, saying, "I have no one else of kindred spirit who will genuinely be concerned [*merimnao*] for your welfare" (2:20). This "concern" for the Philippian church propelled Paul to action. He sent his son in the faith and continually lifted the Philippian church in prayer (1:4). Therefore, in this instance, "concern" is a good and godly thing.

Care

In the twelfth chapter of Paul's first letter to the Corinthians, he described to them the nature and function of the church. He explained that even though believers have a personal relationship with God, they are also united into the corporate family of God within the life of the church. After Paul provided necessary teaching on spiritual gifts and exhorted them to be unified, he shared that God's goal in the church is that "the members may have the same care [*merimnao*] for one another" (1 Corinthians 12:25 ESV). In this instance, "care" is crucial for the unity and health of the body of Christ and is therefore a good and godly thing.

Anxiety and Worry

In at least twelve of the seventeen times the word *merimnao* is used, it is translated either as "anxiety" or "worry." And in each case it is something that the Bible is speaking against. For example, Jesus said, "Do not be anxious" (Matthew 6:25 ESV). In Luke 10:41, Jesus corrected Martha by saying, "Martha, Martha, you are worried and distracted by many things." Paul, in his same letter to the Philippian church, said, "Be anxious for nothing" (Philippians 4:6). In such instances, when the Bible speaks of anxiety and worry, it is referring to something sinful and ungodly that stems from a deficient exercise of faith and misdirected gaze at our problems, fears, and troubles, rather than on God.

Maybe at this point you're asking the question, "So how do I know the difference between godly care and concern and ungodly anxiety, fear, and worry?"

I hope this is a helpful summary:

When Is Merimnao a Good Thing?

+ Jack is a married man with three young boys. After working in the same office for eleven years, Jack discovers that the company that employs him is going out of business. Considering his three hungry young boys to feed and a mortgage to pay, Jack is rightfully concerned (*merimnao*) about finding a new job. Therefore, he takes the necessary steps to create a résumé, knock on doors, and fill out applications, all while praying that God would lead him to an opportunity that would provide for his family. Furthermore, *while* Jack is searching for a job, he is thankful that God has already promised to meet all his needs in Christ Jesus (Philippians 4:19), because "He cares" (1 Peter 5:7). In this case Jack understands that being diligent to look for a job isn't an antonym of reliance on God, nor does he wait to thank God till *after* his prayer is answered, but rather his diligence is the expression of his reliance on God and his thankfulness is the fruit of the settled conviction that God has promised to care, love, and provide for him. Remember what we examined previously? All our anxieties are invitations to draw closer to God by fixating our gaze on who He is. In this case concern is legitimate and healthy and drives us to take action all while expressing our dependency on God.

✦ Jessica loves her daughter. Like all good mothers, Jessica cares (*merimnao*) for her health, her friends, and her future. Because Jessica has a legitimate care for her daughter, she makes it a priority to invest in her and pray for her. There are several unknowns in her daughter's future: *Where will she go to college? Will she go at all? Who will she marry? Will she even marry at all?* All of these unknowns in the future and in the present Jessica casts upon the Lord as she entrusts her precious daughter to her heavenly Father. In this case care is legitimate and godly.

When Does Merimnao Become Sinful?

✦ When our concerns and cares grow so out of control that we lose sight of God's wisdom, sovereignty, and love and, in turn, become paralyzed by the unknown, we become anxious. Often our anxieties may have started as legitimate cares and concerns, but when we attempt to bear our burdens and dwell on our worries and fears, instead of casting them upon the Lord and dwelling on His character, we become sinfully anxious. Furthermore, when we fixate our gaze on our problems and pressures rather than on God, our hearts (and bodies) not only grow anxious, but we also accomplish nothing. We go nowhere. Corrie ten Boom once said, "Worrying is carrying tomorrow's load with today's strength—carrying two days at once. It is moving into tomorrow ahead of time. Worrying does not empty tomorrow of its sorrow—it empties today of its strength."[1] Consider the previous example of Jack, who is looking for a job because of his biblical desire to provide for his family. When Jack's concern is more like a stagnant pool than it is a flowing channel, he becomes sinfully anxious. Rather than being diligent to search for a job and prayerfully depend on God, Jack loses all sense of reliance on God, takes matters entirely into his own hands, and takes his gaze off God's love, wisdom, sovereignty, and provision, and places his gaze firmly on the what ifs and unknowns of life. In this instance Jack's legitimate concern has become a sinful anxiety. Worry is meditation. Whatever we worry about, we fixate on. And when we fixate unduly on our fears, concerns, and cares, we fail to exercise our faith in who God is as our heavenly Father.

+ Additionally, let's consider Jessica and her care for her daughter. Let's say Jessica becomes preoccupied with her daughter's future and becomes crippled with fear over some of the decisions that her daughter is making in the present; her rightful and necessary concern can morph into an ungodly anxiety, wherein she believes that she, as the mother, is the ultimate sovereign over her daughter's life rather than the God who made her. Again, in this case, we see that so many of our anxieties start as rightful and legitimate, but when we carry our burdens instead of casting them onto God, we are in sin. When we are gripped by fear and filled with worry over things we cannot control, we are telling God: "I do not trust You."

Let's say the difference between anxiety/worry from care/concern is akin to the difference between a stagnant pool and a flowing stream. When I was a camp director, I would occasionally go on my off day into Kings Canyon National Park with my friend Harrison. Within the park there were various pools that were consumed with algae because of the water's stagnation and disconnection from the stream. In turn, these waters would grow increasingly cloudy and green throughout the summer. Conversely, there were also flowing streams that contained water that was both drinkable and crystal clear. There was no stagnation in the stream because the water was continually flowing. In that same way, when we worry, our minds are like stagnant pools. We pretend that we are the terminus for our problems and pressures instead of viewing our worries and unknowns as a channel flowing toward God Himself. When we *pool* our anxieties rather than *channel* them toward God, we live as functional atheists. We may claim to believe in God, but when our hearts are weighed down by cares and concerns to the degree that we become anxious about them, Jesus said we are living exactly as the Gentiles, who didn't know God at all (Matthew 6:32).

I say this not to heap shame on those of us who struggle with worry and anxiety but rather so that we might understand that the anxiety the Bible speaks of is not a disease but a sin. I sometimes wonder if there is any category left in the Christian's mind for the reality that there is indeed a sinful anxiety that finds at its root a failure to exercise our faith and fix our gaze on God. Understanding that worry is a sin is not paralyzing; it is freeing! Why? Because only when we grasp that worry is offensive to God will we be able to move forward in confession, repentance, and transformation—which is the pathway to peace.

At times we may not even be aware of the things in our lives that are a recipe for anxiety. Therefore, the good news is that Jesus Himself is the Great Physician. He provides the prognosis, only after He has revealed the true and real diagnosis. He isn't going after the symptoms; He is going after the roots of our anxiety. In Matthew 6:25, Jesus said, "Therefore I tell you, do not be anxious." (ESV). Now, as you may know, when we see the word *therefore* in Scripture, we come to what is one of the most important Bible words. The word functions as a culmination and consequence of what has been previously stated. In this regard, before we continue to examine the prohibition and consequent *prescription* that Jesus gave, we need to review the root causes that the Great Physician calls us to consider. As when the doctor places the stethoscope on your chest and tells you to "breathe," or when the physician asks, "Does it hurt here?" as they make their way toward the pain point, Jesus asks three questions of His followers as He begins to expose the sources of our worry and fear. Jesus asks:

1. Where is your treasure (Matthew 6:19–21)?
2. Where are you looking (Matthew 6:22–23)?
3. Who is your master (Matthew 6:24)?

Where Is Your Treasure?

> "Do not store up for yourselves treasures on earth, where
> moth and rust destroy, and where thieves break in and
> steal. But store up for yourselves treasures in heaven,
> where neither moth nor rust destroys, and where thieves
> do not break in or steal; for where your treasure is,
> there your heart will be also." (Matthew 6:19–21)

Between the ages of one and eighteen, I'm not entirely sure if I ever went to the doctor, other than for the seemingly annual accident that required stitches (the '90s were different). But at twenty-five years old, I went to see the doctor so I could get an opinion about some nagging pain on the top of my foot—WebMD had told me I had tendonitis, and when are they ever wrong? The podiatrist examined my foot and then my leg itself and then within a matter of minutes sent me to get an X-ray. After the results came back, the doctor told me the X-rays revealed a break, but, to my surprise, the break was not in my foot but somewhere else: my knee was *broken*. I remember injuring my knee (long story) but didn't think much of it. But now, after compensating for the pain for so long, I noticed the pain in another part of my body. The pain in my foot was *real*, but it wasn't the *root* problem.

Similarly, Jesus illustrates that the worries of our minds often find their roots somewhere else: our treasures. Far from parachuting into the topic of anxiety, Jesus begins by saying, "Do not store up for yourselves treasures on earth. . . . But store up for yourselves treasures in heaven . . . for where your treasure is, there your heart will be also" (Matthew 6:19–21). Four verses later He says, "Therefore I tell you, do not be anxious" (v. 25, ESV). So what He says in verses 19–21 has massive implications for what He will say in verse 25. When speaking about our treasures, Jesus is talking about what we prioritize, what we value, and what grabs our affection. He is talking about money, but He refers to more than mere money when He addresses our treasure. Why? Because there can be no money in our bank accounts and yet our hearts can be full of earthly treasures. Maybe the treasures of our hearts are not even ours in actuality but in potentiality—we treasure that which we don't yet possess but have already established on the heart's pedestal.

When Jesus addresses our treasures, He is not necessarily referring to our possessions but to our *attitude* toward our possessions.[2] A man can possess great degrees of wealth and yet hold it with an open hand and therefore be free from "treasuring" his wealth. Conversely, a man can have little to his name and yet be obsessive over what he desires and greedy with what he already has. The fact that Jesus' exhortation on earthly treasures is given not merely to the monetarily elite but to the common folk of Israel draws our attention to a certain reality: the "have-nots" are just as susceptible to treasuring earthly things as those with deep pockets. Are possessions a bad thing? No! "Every good and perfect gift" is from God (James 1:17 NIV), and "no good thing does He withhold from those who walk uprightly" (Psalm 84:11 ESV).

Jesus is not the enemy of possessions; He is the giver and the granter of them. Yet Jesus makes a clear distinction between the things we hold with an open hand and the things we grasp with a clenched fist. Jesus explains to His anxious followers that when we take a good thing (such as possessions) and make it ultimate in our affections, that thing becomes an idol, and therein lies the perfect recipe for anxiety. *Treasure* is an all-inclusive term. It may mean money, it may mean possessions, but it may be sports, academics, prestige, reputability, your husband, wife, children; it may be something you don't possess and yet desire, or it may be something you do possess that you are afraid to lose.

When we treasure the *gift* more than the *Giver* Himself, our hearts become restless, our legitimate concerns become worries, and often our worries drive us toward despair. Good things can often become idols, and when they do, God's children become gripped with anxious fear. For example, is a pastor's care for his congregation a bad thing? Of course not! But when the affirmation, praise, and respect of the congregation become so prominent in the pastor's mind that they turn into the pastor's treasure, the pastor has turned a good thing into an idol. The examples are numerous, but you would only have to use your imagination to make the illustration personal to your own life.

How do we lay up treasures on earth? Well, very simple: We devote our lives to them. We elevate and exalt our relationships, possessions, status, and position above God Himself. Furthermore, the moment we obtain what we had imagined as our dream house, job, or spouse is the moment we become afraid to lose it. Why? Because moths eat, things rust, robbers steal, stocks prices fall, jobs are insecure, and life is unpredictable (Matthew 6:19). The surest path to anxiety is to forget that we are pilgrims just passing through this life, and in turn, we stop living for the "better country" (Hebrews 11:16) that is to come and start obsessing over our lives in the here and now. Fashions change. Minds dim. Faces wrinkle. "The most beautiful flower begins to die the moment you pluck it."[3] This world is passing away, so Jesus asks us: *Why would you live for it?* If we do live for this world, of course we will be anxious, because everything in this world is fleeting, fragile, and unpredictable. But if we set up for ourselves treasures in heaven, where neither moth nor rust destroys and where thieves don't break in and steal (Matthew 6:19), we will live our lives with a "blessed detachment from this world."[4]

Jesus asks us these questions through His living Word: *What do you treasure? Who do you treasure? Is what you treasure making you anxious? Why would you treasure things that will rot instead of laying up treasures in heaven, where an "imperishable, undefiled, and unfading"* (1 Peter 1:4 ESV) *inheritance awaits you?*

Where Are You Looking?

> "The eye is the lamp of the body; so then, if your eye
> is clear, your whole body will be full of light. But if
> your eye is bad, your whole body will be full of dark-
> ness. If then the light that is in you is darkness, how
> great is the darkness!" (Matthew 6:22–23)

Before Jesus addressed the subject of anxiety in Matthew 6:25, the Good Physician exposed some of the underlying causes. Jesus detailed that the despairing in heart and the anxious of mind need to examine what they look at with their eyes. Although Jesus was still addressing the topic of our treasures (vv. 19–21), He explained to His followers that there is a historic channel by which something takes root in the heart. First, we look at it with our eyes and then fixate on it with our minds, and then it becomes an idol in our hearts.

In our hypersexualized, narcissistic, self-focused, self-loving, immoral, and rumormongering culture, people flood their minds with images, gossip, and news stories that perpetuate their anxiety. The average person spends seven hours a day looking at their smartphone, computer, and television screens, and, sadly, much of the content consumed, if it is not overtly sinful, does not contribute to "taking every thought captive" in order that we might honor Christ (2 Corinthians 10:5).[5] Our devices are indeed wonderful tools, but so are hammers—and great tools can be terrifying weapons when not stewarded appropriately. These wonderful tools that allow us to communicate, search, and stream can also hollow our souls and pulverize our minds.

In examining the root causes of our anxiety, Jesus asks, "Where are you looking?" Our eyes are not disconnected from our minds and hearts. Jesus explained that they are wedded together by saying, "The eye is the lamp of the body." What you look at, what you set your gaze on, is the window into your soul. So Jesus is asking you through His living Word, *What do you look at? What are you feeding your mind with through the vehicle of your eye?*

In our perverse, pornographic, and materialistic world, it's no wonder that so many people struggle with anxiety.

One recent study indicates the "significant relationship between mental health and porn consumption."[6] Many teens *and* adults today use pornography to cope with their anxiety and depression, and yet, in doing so, they only fuel greater degrees of the fears and emotions they seek to suppress. The link between pornography consumption and soaring anxiety rates is true in general, but it ought to be especially true among those who claim to be children of God. Pornography is consumed under the false veil of anonymity and the thought: *No one else knows.* These thoughts tend to isolate us not only from one another but also from God. Pornography presents the constant allure of experiencing forbidden fruit that grows on new trees every single day. But as it was for Adam and Eve, the immediate result of consuming forbidden fruit is fear, shame, and anxiety.

Sexual sin corrupts our souls and wreaks havoc on our minds. If you're a Christian, you are a temple of the Holy Spirit, and when you operate in unrepentant sin, you grieve God (Ephesians 4:30) and rob yourself of the joy and peace that comes from Him (Psalm 51:12).

The age of anxious people gets younger and younger, and many secular psychologists have linked the rise in anxiety to the rise in porn consumption. The average age of exposure to pornography today is eleven years old. Ninety-four percent of children will view porn by the age of fourteen. This is a tragedy in and of itself and not disconnected from the subject of anxiety. Why? Because Jesus said in Matthew 5:8, "Blessed are the pure in heart, for they will see God." But many today pollute their minds and share their bodies outside God's design and in violation of God's Word, and, in doing so, they rob themselves of God's peace and present all the ingredients for an anxious mind.

Although pornography promises an "escape," all it truly does is perpetuate the prison of anxiety and despair.

But whether it is pornography or the latest fashion trends, what we look at with our eyes becomes the focus of our minds, and the focus of our minds becomes the treasure within our hearts.

I love these words from hymn writer and poet Helen Lemmel (1863–1961):

> Turn your eyes upon Jesus,
> look full in His wonderful face,
> and the things of earth will grow strangely dim,
> in the light of His glory and grace.

If you want a realignment of your treasure, you must realign your vision, you must redirect your gaze. Jesus asks you, *Where are you looking?* Why? Because the worries of our minds are often the fruits of where we set our gaze.

Who Is Your Master?

*"No one can serve two masters; for either he will hate the one
and love the other, or he will be devoted to one and despise the
other. You cannot serve God and wealth."* (Matthew 6:24)

Every master is a totalitarian. They demand all of you. People
dupe themselves into thinking they can serve two masters, but
Jesus said you cannot. You cannot fear the Lord and serve graven
images (2 Kings 17:23–41). Love cannot be mixed. Service cannot
be divided. Of course, when Jesus talked about what or whom we
serve, He was speaking in relation to our hearts. Where our allegiance lies is often where our anxieties find their root. In considering
that which masters us, may I suggest some soul surgery? Setting a
broken bone is painful but it leads to healing. Likewise, probing our
own heart can promote pain, but it's the necessary pain that leads
to growth. In relation to that which masters us, Jesus was referring
not only to literal masters but to the figurative ones that we submit
our lives to.

1. Have You Been Mastered by Bitterness?

Has someone sinned against you? Are you holding on to a
grudge? Is your heart full of resentment? Often, we want justice,
maybe even vengeance on those who have hurt us or hurt the ones
we love. I once talked with a woman who said she was plagued by
anxiety. I asked her some questions and she relayed to me that her
anxiety had been amplified ever since she caught her husband in an
affair. She had been suspicious of his many business trips over the
years and had hired a private investigator to follow him. On one
occasion her fears were realized when she followed her husband to
the airport. There she witnessed that it was not her husband's business partners that greeted him at the airport but his secretary. He

had lied and deceived her for years. A year later they got a divorce. The marriage was over, she had tried to move on, yet there was something she would not let go of—her bitterness. She hated her husband; this bitterness was planted and, consequently, a root system of anxiety spread throughout her soul. Of course, her husband had been wrong, very wrong! But we can respond to wrong in the wrong ways. Bitterness deteriorates our souls, but there is much freedom in forgiveness.

Bitterness produces anxiety, but forgiveness offers healing. The author of Hebrews put it this way: "See to it that no one comes short of the grace of God; that no root of bitterness springing up causes trouble, and by it many be defiled" (Hebrews 12:15). The follower of Christ forgives others, not only because an unforgiving heart produces bitterness and, consequently, anxiety, but also because "Christ also has forgiven you" (Ephesians 4:32). Jesus forgave those who beat Him, spit on Him, and crucified Him—in His final moments He prayed, "Father, forgive them" (Luke 23:34)! Are you holding on to bitterness? Then confess that to Christ and ask Him for His power to enable you to forgive just as He has forgiven you.

2. Are You Harboring Unconfessed Sin?

The believer is no longer under sin's reign but is still susceptible to the temptations of the flesh. And when we indulge, harbor, and relish things that Jesus died to save us from, our souls reap the consequences. The man after God's own heart said that when he kept silent about his sin, his bones wasted away through his groaning all day long (Psalm 32:3). David said, "For day and night Your hand was heavy upon me; my vitality was drained away as with the fever heat of summer" (v. 4). Much more could be said here, but our souls are not strong enough to bear the gigantic load of unconfessed and unrepented sin. Sin is sapping. Disobedience is draining. Rebellion promises to invigorate, but in the end it only enervates. When we fail to walk in obedience to God's Word and fail to confess that sin to God that we might receive the promised forgiveness and cleansing He offers (1 John 1:9), we sear our consciences and suck the life out of our souls. Those who are saved cannot lose their salvation, but do you know what they can lose? Their joy. For this reason, David, after confessing his sin, prayed, "Restore unto me the joy of thy salvation" (Psalm 51:12 KJV).

Who Do You Believe?

After addressing some of the root causes of anxiety, Jesus provided the ultimate cause of worry and fear: unbelief. After proclaiming a prohibition against anxiety in Matthew 6:25, Jesus continued, "But if God so clothes the grass of the field, which is alive today and tomorrow is thrown into the furnace, will He not much more clothe you? You of little faith!" (Matthew 6:30). In the previous chapter, we addressed some of the natural causes that contribute to our anxiety, but the physical and temperamental causes do not disqualify the truth of Scripture in which Jesus revealed that all worry finds at its root a lack of faith in God as Father—not in the sense that we no longer believe *in* God but that we no longer *believe God*. When preaching to His anxious followers, Jesus rebuked the littleness (not the absence) of their faith. His rebukes, however, were never spoken in outbursts of anger but always given consistently with His heart of love. He didn't berate the anxious like a ruthless coach to an ineffective player; He reproved as a loving father toward the cherished child.

Unbelief in God's promise to provide can prompt anxiety about your finances and your future. Unbelief in God's sovereignty can function as the recipe for anxiety when you grasp at the illusion of your own control instead of entrusting everything in your life unto God's control. Unbelief in God's love can lead to a loss of satisfaction in that love (Psalm 90:14), so much so that you seek satisfaction from the world rather than from your heavenly Father (1 John 2:14–16). Worry is the offspring of the mind not actively governed by faith in our Father.

The adversary of our souls will use physical infirmity, natural temperament, exhaustion, loneliness, and previous trauma to propel us toward anxiety and depression. As we observed in the story of Job, Satan will use all the tools at his disposal to make us doubt God's goodness and control. He will employ every resource to sap us of the joy that comes from Christ. The devil wants to steal our joy by promising us counterfeit pleasures. He wants us to doubt the truth we affirm and the God we know. The first question ever asked in human history is "Did God really say . . . ?" (Genesis 3:1 NIV). The devil is a cunning and strategic hunter of souls. He knows that trust and peace grow in the garden of faith and that depression and anxiety flourish in the fields of doubt.

In this chapter, we have considered the spiritual root causes of our anxiety. Jesus asks us four questions: (1) Where is your treasure? (2) Where are you looking? (3) Who is your master? (4) Who do you believe?

Now that we have examined the root causes of our anxiety, in the next chapter we will begin to consider the ultimate cure the Great Physician provides—*faith*. Maybe in your mind "faith" is synonymous with "belief"; this may be true to some degree, but when Jesus discussed faith with those who *already* believed in Him, it was not so much that He was telling them to affirm the existence of God or to acknowledge His power. Jesus was calling them to do something else entirely—according to the Great Physician, faith has everything to do with our *gaze*. And for us to fix our eyes on our heavenly Father, we must come to know His character and come to grips with the reality that we aren't merely to acknowledge the facts but to *consider* the character of our loving and sovereign God.

Reflection Questions

1. What are some differences between concern, care, and anxiety in the Bible? Why is distinguishing anxiety from a godly concern important? How can godly concern turn into ungodly anxiety?

2. Jesus connected anxiety to misplaced "treasures" in Matthew 6:19. What are some of the people, ambitions, ideas, or things in your life—which may not be bad in and of themselves—that may be elevated to the degree of treasure? Might they be contributing to your worry?

3. Jesus said that what we see with our eyes has a direct effect on what we worry about—"the eye is the lamp of the body" (Matthew 6:22–23). The eye is the window into your soul and, therefore, has a dramatic influence on the thoughts within your mind. What are things that you watch, read, or look at that take your gaze off God and affix you to the things of this world?

CHAPTER 5

Your Mind Matters

I have a theory: if you have a personal name for your car, I'm going to go out on a limb and guess that your car is *barely* alive.

Let me explain.

I've rarely met someone with a car named "Pearl," "Stella," or "Jim-Bob" who is driving a brand-new Toyota Tacoma or Ford Expedition. Those personal names are typically reserved for a beat-up Volkswagen Beetle, a thirty-year-old Honda Civic, an old Pontiac, or, in the case of the car my dad drove when I was growing up, a 1986 Chrysler LeBaron we affectionately named "the Classic."

One time in the 1990s, my dad was driving us to school and we heard a clunk, clunk, clank! We looked behind us and there, steaming in the snow, was our muffler. We took it home, rammed it back into place, and thought, *It'll drive another day.* Another time, the carpet on the interior ceiling started peeling off so that it hung like a curtain and would impede my dad's vision when he was driving. Naturally, my brother and I did what any other kids would do: we borrowed our teacher's staple gun and stapled the carpet back to the ceiling. The list goes on and on. Whether it was our accessing the back seat by crawling from the front seat (because the back doors didn't open) or our banging the radiator with a hammer to start the car, our relationship with the Classic was defined by temporary fixes. These "remedies" never solved the real problems but simply masked and suppressed the real issues at hand.

A Lasting Remedy

The world's approach to the subject of worry is often akin to my family's relationship with the Classic. Quick fixes to help us *manage*. The problem is that the "fixes" the world offers aren't really fixes at all; they are temporary alleviations at best. Momentary distractions. But shoving worry down isn't making it go away. Worry rarely takes a day off—it will be back tomorrow.

I'm guessing your heart longs for something more than symptom suppression. I know mine does. What we yearn for is a peace that endures. Our world is broken, and *we* are broken; therefore, the peace we long for cannot be of ourselves, it cannot be *natural*—it must be *supernatural*. Maybe you acknowledge the reality that you need God's help to take away your anxiety and have prayed, *God, take my anxiety away*—which is good, as long as the prayer is conjoined to an understanding that God doesn't simply want to *remove* your worry; He wants to *replace* your worry with trust. Praying *God, take away my worry* is not the same thing as praying, *God, help me trust You as I feed my mind with the truth of Your Word and meditate on Your matchless character. Fix my mind and set my gaze on Your love, wisdom, and sovereignty and give me a peace that can come only from You.* The opposite of anxiety is not the absence thereof but the presence of something only God can provide: "perfect peace" (Isaiah 26:3).

When Jesus responds to His anxious followers on the Mount

of Beatitudes, He does not offer a coping mechanism or a quick fix for *managing* anxiety. On the contrary, as the Great Physician, He provides a powerful cure. Jesus gathers those who are worried about their lives; the occupation of Rome; the battle for bread; the future of their relationships, homes, and finances and tells them, "Do not be anxious" (Matthew 6:25 ESV). Thankfully, Jesus doesn't stop there—He then instructs them to *think* on the character of our heavenly Father. Far from the shallow anti-intellectualism that we see among many churches today, the Christian faith requires *deep thinking*. And, to prompt His anxious followers to think, Jesus gives an unforgettable object lesson that detailed not only the character of God but also the path forward for those who are anxious.

Consider the Lilies

After exposing the roots of anxiety and providing the prohibition against it by saying "Do not be anxious," Jesus began to prescribe the cure. As the greatest teacher in human history, Jesus spoke authoritatively as God yet compassionately and earnestly to His own. Jesus did not teach in the dry, monotone style of a lecturer; He taught with object lessons that capture our attention and compel our contemplation. Jesus wanted His followers to grasp what He was saying, so He used imagery to drive His message home. In His magnum opus on anxiety and God's character, Jesus first instructed His followers to "look at the birds" (Matthew 6:26) and then told them to "consider the lilies" (Matthew 6:28 NKJV).

We will examine in a moment why Jesus used these object lessons, but for now I want you to consider what it means to be made in the image of God (Genesis 1:26). After all, isn't God a spirit (John 4:24)? So how can we reflect His image? He's not brown haired, brown eyed, and six feet tall (or, in my case, five eleven and a half), right?

The Bible teaches that we are made in God's image, not because we share His physical appearance, but because we possess rational and relational qualities that no other creatures share. As His image bearers, we can reason as He does. Yes, other creatures can think—dogs can be trained to grab a soda (or "pop" if you're from the Midwest) from the fridge, dolphins can jump through hoops, and birds can build nests, but do you know what they cannot do? Build an iPhone or compose a symphony. Animals operate by instinct and human beings by intelligence, logic, and reason. Why? Because man is made in the image of God—we are *thinking* creatures. Grasping this reality is crucial to our discussion, because within our minds lie both the problem and the solution to our anxiety.

The fall of man in Genesis 3 resulted in drastic consequences for our minds. Not only did Adam's sin affect the world in which we live, but it also affected our minds with which we think. Our minds that were made to behold God's goodness, love, and glory are now, outside of Christ, darkened, futile, and depraved. No longer does the natural man have a bent *toward* God but rather a hardwiring of hostility *against* Him (Romans 1:21; Colossians 1:21). And what darkened minds need is the light of the revelation of God so that we might know Him. Although Christians receive a new heart at the moment of our justification (Ezekiel 36:26), our minds are continually and progressively renewed over time until we meet Jesus face-to-face. We will talk more about justification in the next chapter, but for now it is crucial to understand that Christianity, above all the other religions in the world, places a supreme value on the *mind*.

In every category of holiness and Christlikeness, how we grow as a Christian necessitates the stewardship and transformation of the way we think and where we set our minds. Observe for a moment this great theme in the Bible:

- "Do not be conformed to this world, but be transformed by the renewing of your *mind*" (Romans 12:2).
- "Be renewed in the spirit of your *mind*" (Ephesians 4:23).
- "Set your *mind* on the things above" (Colossians 3:2).
- "Love the Lord your God with all your heart . . . soul . . . *mind* and . . . strength" (Mark 12:30).[1]

Bottom line: the Christian life is a battle for the mind. If you want to grow in your trust in God and experience the peace that can come only from God, then you must learn to fix your mind on Him. Consider the words of Isaiah 26:3: "You keep him in perfect peace whose *mind* is stayed on you, because he trusts in you" (ESV, emphasis added). The promise of God's Word is that those who "stay" their minds on God are kept in perfect peace. Do you want the peace of God to "guard your hearts and your minds in Christ Jesus" (Philippians 4:7)? Then you need to prepare your mind for action (1 Peter 1:13). As your mind goes, so goes the entirety of your spiritual life. Your will and your feelings are (except in rare cases) subservient to your mind. Therefore, the sum and substance of your Christian life is what you think about. Proverbs 23:7 puts it this way: "For as he thinks within himself, so he is." Small thoughts of God and shallow levels of intimacy with Him will always result in a small degree of peace and shallow levels of trust. Your stability amid the storms of life is in direct proportion to the degree that your mind is fixed on God (Colossians 3:1).

While imprisoned in a Roman jail, Paul penned these words: "Be anxious for nothing, but in everything by prayer and supplication, with thanksgiving, let your requests be made known to God; and the peace of God, which surpasses all understanding, will guard your hearts and minds through Christ Jesus" (Philippians 4:6–7 NKJV). Paul said, *Substitute worry with prayer, and despair with thanksgiving!* Surely, this is much easier said than done. How can

I be anxious for nothing? Paul told us how in the following verse: "Finally, brothers, whatever is true, whatever is honorable, whatever is just, whatever is pure, whatever is lovely, whatever is commendable, if there is any excellence, if there is anything worthy of praise, think about these things" (Philippians 4:8 ESV). The prescription Scripture provides for us is not simply to *remove* our anxiety but to *replace* our anxious thoughts with thoughts of whatever is true, honorable, just, pure, lovely, and excellent. God responded to Elijah, Moses, Job, and His anxious followers on the Mount of Beatitudes by, first and foremost, asking them questions. Why? Because questions solicit self-examination, they prompt a pondering of God's character, they engender a consideration of who God is. Questions . . . force us to *think*.

Therefore, God asks His anxious followers:

+ What are you doing? (1 Kings 19:13).
+ Is not life more than food and the body more than clothing? (Matthew 6:25).
+ Who made the human mouth? (Exodus 4:11).
+ Why are you downcast? (Psalm 42:11 NIV).

This introductory step to healing is consistent throughout Scripture. *Think. Think. Think.* As Jesus taught, He not only asked questions but also employed illustrations. He beckoned his worried followers to "look at the birds of the air," then said, "They do not sow, nor reap nor gather into barns, and yet your heavenly Father feeds them. Are you not worth much more than they?" (Matthew 6:26). Likewise, Jesus told His followers to "consider the lilies of the field," for, He continued, "they do not labor nor do they spin thread for cloth, yet I say to you that not even Solomon in all his glory clothed himself like one of these. But if God so clothes the grass of the field, which is alive today and tomorrow is thrown into the furnace, will He not much more clothe you? You of little faith!" (6:28–30 NKJV). Here Jesus argued from the lesser to the greater. In philosophy, this strategy is known as "a fortiori" because it forces us to recognize that if A is true, how much more certainly is B true? Jesus was compelling them to consider *if God feeds, provides for, cares for, and sustains the birds, how much more will He feed, provide for, care for, and sustain those who are made in His image and whom He has purchased with the blood of His one and only Son?*

Jesus will lovingly chide the anxious and say, "You of little faith," and yet, in doing so, He reveals to us the very means by which we overcome our anxiety and fear. If anxiety is the product of "little faith," then the antidote to anxiety is feeding our faith in our heavenly Father. Now, at this point you may respond and say: "But I've already placed my faith in God. How can my faith be little?" This is a legitimate question to ask. The truth is that Christians are saved by believing in the person and work of Jesus Christ (Romans 10:9). This cannot be denied. For the follower of Christ, however, faith is not a once-upon-a-time *thing* but an everyday exercise. And to Jesus, living by faith has everything to do with where we set our gaze.

Gazing at God

When I was a child, I played Little League baseball. I'll never forget it. Our team went 0–16. Winless. I, however, didn't have too shabby of a season (if I can say so myself). My dad and I used to have batting practice at the nearby junior high, and he gave me some valuable lessons about America's pastime. The first lesson was this: When you are trying to hit the ball, you do not keep your eyes on the bat—you keep your eyes where? On the ball. This is fundamental, but it is the first rung of the baseball ladder.

Similarly, for the Christian whose faith is "striking out" and is constantly badgered by worry, the first thing to understand is that our faith grows not as we keep our eyes on faith itself but as we fix our eyes on Jesus Christ. In the same way it would be impossible to hit the ball while keeping our eyes on the bat, it would be impossible for us to grow in our faith if we kept our focus *on our faith* rather than on Jesus *Himself*.

When Jesus rebukes His worried followers for the littleness of their faith (Matthew 6:30), He means two primary things: (1) they had a small view of who God actually was, and (2) even if they affirmed and acknowledged different elements of His character, they had failed to appropriately meditate on the truths they affirmed. Instead, they chose to dwell on the worries and anxieties that bombarded them. In turn, their faith had become "little." According to Jesus, the antidote to anxiety is not merely a thoughtful glance toward the prohibition to "not be anxious about anything" (Philippians 4:6) but a contemplation of all the reasons why. Why should we *not* be anxious? How can I stop *being* anxious? What can buoy my despairing heart when I feel as if I am drowning in a sea of suffering? Faith—and by "faith" I mean *gazing at God*. To behold God in His Word requires that we meditate on its truth and, in doing so, dwell on His character. Unfortunately, Eastern religion has hijacked the word *meditation* from Scripture, which necessitates that we revisit the term to better understand the initial remedy that God prescribes.

Biblical Meditation

Meditation, according to Scripture, is a critical discipline and duty that weds doctrine with practice and integrates biblical truth to our lives. Far from meditation being an *emptying* of our minds, as Eastern religion instructs, meditation is a *filling* up of our minds with the truth found in God's Word. My friend Harry always refers to meditation as the process by which we "chew the cud" of Scripture. I don't think it's presumptuous for me to guess that few of you are cattle farmers and that the phrase "chew the cud" might be unfamiliar to you—so here's a little reminder: A cow has four compartments in its stomach, which it needs to break down the tough and coarse food it eats. When a cow first eats, it chews the food just enough to swallow it. The swallowed food that remains largely unchewed travels to the rumen, where it is stored until later. The rumen is like a large fermentation vat that contains bacteria that break down and soften the food into what is called *cud*. The cud is then sent back to the cow's mouth where it is re-chewed before going back down into the stomach to be fully digested.

This, according to my friend Harry, is what it means to meditate.

Too often we attempt to swallow whole the truth, which disables proper digestion of the spiritual nutrition in God's Word. As a result, we can confess the truth and confirm the truth and yet still be a stranger to the comfort that God intends to supply us through His Word. Meditation ensures that the truth we have studied and heard does not slip but stays in our minds. The English Puritan Thomas Watson once said, "Without meditation the truth of God will not stay with us; the heart is hard, and the memory slippery, and without meditation all is lost; meditation imprints and fastens a truth in the mind. . . . As a hammer drives a nail to the head, so meditation drives a truth to the heart. Without meditation the word preached may increase notion, not affection."[2] We are all prone to practice a superficial Christianity in which we ski over the rich depths of God's Word rather than scuba dive into its depths. The practice of meditation shatters superficial faith and shallow thinking. Jesus tells us to "consider," Paul tells us to "think," and Peter tells us to "prepare our minds for action." Remember, whatever shapes your mind shapes your life. Are you anxious? The Bible asks, *What are you filling your mind with? Do you feed your mind entertainment, worldliness, lust, pandemonium, and all the chaos of the unknown? Or do you feed your mind with whatever is pure, lovely, honorable, and true?*

"Think on These Things"

To the anxious, Jesus conveys that our worry is rooted in a deficient understanding of the nature of our heavenly Father. He is saying to you through His Word, *If only you really knew what God is like! Then you would understand that there is never a reason on earth for you to be worried.*

In the chapters to come, we will explore a number of the attributes of God that provide comfort, and my aim is to encourage not just acknowledgment of these truths but transformation of the *mind*. This requires meditation. We too often hear and read Scripture but rarely chew and digest the truths found within it. As a result, we can confirm the existence of God's power and sovereignty but be strangers to the experience those realities ought to produce in our hearts. Oswald Chambers referred to meditation as a "spiritual concentration" by which superficial faith is vanquished and deep faith begins.[3] To meditate on God's character means that we deliberately set apart time to think about and consider who God is and then make it the habit of our lives to dwell on His Word and be in prayer throughout the day. It's no wonder why, in our fast-paced lives, people are more anxious than ever. We have all but eliminated our need and ability to ponder. In doing so, we have sabotaged our spiritual lives. We cannot deepen our faith in God unless we learn to digest the truth about God in His word. When we do, God becomes all the more real to us! Over and over again throughout the Psalms, we read that the psalmist meditated on the Word of God, not as an academic or intellectual exercise, but as the necessary means to the desired end—knowing God. David Saxton, in his book *God's Battle Plan for the Mind*, wrote, "Just as there would be no true healing from a surgery without a serious commitment to physical rest, so there is no spiritual healing without a commitment to meditation."[4]

The Enemy of the Mind

Prior to an individual's conversion, Satan operates in one predominant fashion: "The god of this world has blinded *the minds* of the unbelieving so that they might not see the light of the gospel of the glory of Christ, who is the image of God" (2 Corinthians 4:4, emphasis added). Although Satan no longer exercises authority over the Christian who has been given the "mind of Christ" (1 Corinthians 2:16), he can still leverage the tools at his disposal to prevent us from thinking deeply about God. He uses distraction, busyness, doubt, sin, and slothfulness to keep us from gazing at God. Satan cannot take you from God's hand, but he can cleverly attempt to rob you of God's peace. He does not mind if you hear the truth as long as you do not chew and digest it. He does not want your mind actively engaging the truth of God; he desires that your mind be stayed upon the problems, chaos, and unknowns in this world. If not, he is perfectly content that your mind be idle. Why? Because an idle mind is the devil's playground. If you are not filling your mind with truth, he will find a way to fill it with lies.

In his letter to the Ephesian church, Paul said that the Christian life is a battle. No one said following Jesus would be easy. In fact, it is impossible to live the Christian life in our own strength. Paul detailed that "our struggle is not against flesh and blood, but against the rulers, against the powers, against the world forces of this darkness, against the spiritual forces of wickedness in the heavenly places" (Ephesians 6:12). Satan strategizes and schemes against the children of God. Sun Tzu once wrote that knowing your enemy is the first step in planning for battle, and the Christian likewise must understand that there is an actual evil being named Satan who desires to rob you of God's peace and blind you from seeing God's character. It would be a mistake to become obsessed with the reality of Satan and find a demon under every rock, but it would also be a mistake to not consider that Satan prowls like a "roaring lion, seeking someone to devour" (1 Peter 5:8). If this is the case, what can we do? How can we protect ourselves from a supernatural being who desires to destroy us?

We must take up the full armor of God.

Paul said, "Be strong in the Lord and in the strength of His might. Put on the full armor of God, so that you will be able to stand firm against the schemes of the devil" (Ephesians 6:10–11). The armor you wear has to do with the way you gird your mind for battle: with the "belt of truth" (v. 14 NIV), the "breastplate of righteousness" (v. 14), the "gospel of peace" (v. 15), the "shield of faith" (v. 16), and the "helmet of salvation" (v. 17). You are in a battle—that much cannot be denied, and you will lose the battle against anxiety and worry (and every other sin, for that matter) if you do not "prepare your minds for action" (1 Peter 1:13).

To an ancient warrior the prospect of going into battle without a sword and shield would be unthinkable. And yet there are millions of Christians who go into battle every day without picking up their armor and weapons in the spiritual battles we face. As I write, I'm reminded of Corrie ten Boom's observation that in the armor that God provides there is no protection for the back, because there are no deserters in the Lord's army, only fighters.[5]

The fight of faith takes place in our minds, and only when we meditate on God's truth and God's promises and seek Him in prayer will we be safe from the temptations of our own flesh and from whatever darts Satan throws our way. A ten-minute "quiet time" cannot equip us for the sixteen-hour battle we face each day. That would be akin to taking a thirty-second shower and then proceeding to roll around in the mud for hours. Believers are to meditate "day and night" (Psalm 1:2)—and what's the promise if we do? Psalm 1:3 tells us that we will become like the man who is "like a tree planted by streams of water, which yields its fruit in its season, and its leaf does not wither; and in whatever he does, he prospers."

God's Perfect Peace

In 1876, Frances Ridley Havergal wrote these words after studying Isaiah 26:3:

> Like a river glorious is God's perfect peace,
> over all victorious in its bright increase:
> perfect, yet still flowing fuller every day;
> perfect, yet still growing deeper all the way.
> Trusting in the Father, hearts are fully blest,
> finding, as he promised, perfect peace and rest.
> Hidden in the hollow of his mighty hand,
> where no harm can follow, in his strength we stand.
> We may trust him fully all for us to do;
> those who trust him wholly find him wholly true.

You could be the richest person in the world, but if you don't have the peace of God, you are poor. But if you fix your mind on God, peace like a river will gush into the reservoir of your heart and mind.

—————— **Reflection Questions** ——————

1. Why does Satan attack our minds? How does he do this? What are the thoughts and accusations he brings against us that might cause us to despair? What armor does God provide for the Christian to ensure that we can stand tall? Read Ephesians 6:10–24.

2. Read Philippians 4:8 and Colossians 3:1–2. What does Paul tell us to meditate or set our minds on? What would it look like in practice if we were to set our minds on things that are above, noble, excellent, pure, and so forth?

3. What is meditation? Why is merely reading Scripture not enough to sustain and equip us in the battle against worry? What are ways to implement a habit of chewing the cud of God's Word?

PART II

Our Loving Father

CHAPTER 6

Knowing *Abba*

When I was growing up, every night my dad would sit down on the floor and read us stories. Bedtime was *story time*. He would make up voices, talk in accents, and hush and raise his voice to draw us in. Whenever he sensed our attention lapsing, he would say, "Oh wow, you won't believe what happens next . . . should I tell you?" We'd all scream, "Tell us!" My dad once told me, "The world belongs to those who read." Ever since then I've been a reader. Novels, biographies, Teddy Roosevelt's journals, you name it, I'll read it. That is, everything except for science fiction (I have my limits, okay?). Although we live in a world where people commonly use the term *life-changing* to describe a turkey sandwich or a recent movie, there are very few things and even fewer books that I would categorize as "life-changing." But if I had to compile a list of my life-changing reads, J. I. Packer's book *Knowing God* would be at the top of it.

I first read Packer's book at the age of nineteen, and, coincidently, my life was forever changed when I read chapter 19 in his book. In the opening line of the chapter, Packer asked, "What is a Christian? The question can be answered in many ways, but the richest answer I know is that a Christian is one who has God as Father."[1] There are so many ways people define Christianity, but Packer said that Christianity, at its core, is a relationship with God as Father. Packer continued, "If you want to judge how well a person understands Christianity, find out how much he makes of the thought of being God's child, and having God as his Father. . . . 'Father' is the Christian name for God."[2] If you are a Christian, the most important thing about you is your depth of conviction and breadth of understanding when you say, *God is my heavenly Father.* And if this is true for every believer, Jesus will say it is especially true for those who are anxious. According to the Great Physician Himself, the surest antidote to anxiety and worry is to know God as "Father" and to cast your cares onto Him.

Perfect Peace

Jesus' teaching on anxiety draws our attention to a reality that may be assumed but nevertheless needs to be addressed: the Father's children are the only people on earth who can experience the Father's peace. This makes sense, right? You cannot possess the peace *of* God if you are not at peace *with* God through Jesus Christ. This bears repeating: the Bible offers no peace or comfort to anyone who does not know God as Father because they have not known Jesus Christ, God's Son, as Savior. Every ounce of the Christian's hope in our dark, troubled, and uncertain world is moored to our identity as children of God. Therefore, for the person who does not possess this assurance, there are thousands (if not millions) of reasons to be anxious. The world we live in is full of uncertainty, death, and disease, and countless billions spend their lives estranged from the God who made them and to whom they will give an account (Hebrews 9:27). It's no surprise that the fear of death is one of the greatest anxieties of the modern era. Why? Because the modern man and woman has no confidence in their eternal state after they die. Their eternal future is unknown, their lives in the present are uncertain, and their God-given consciences testify against them (Ecclesiastes 3:11; Romans 2:15).

Our anxieties grow in the garden of life's unknowns: "What shall we eat or drink? What shall we wear for clothing?" To fight anxiety you must first root your faith in something sure: God is your Father. If you have already placed your faith in Christ and have the assurance that God is your Father, then listen again as Jesus tells you in His Word to rehearse this reality daily and to ground your faith here. I grew up praying "Dear heavenly Father," yet for many years my heart was a stranger to the amazing truth I testified with my lips. Some of the most anxious people on earth are those who grew up declaring great truths about God but are foreigners to the truths they express (Matthew 15:8). What both the seasoned saint and baby believer need is a rehearsal of the gospel and a rooting of our minds in the truth of our identities as children of the Father. If you think this initial cornerstone is too basic, I encourage you to think *again*. The predominant thrust of the rest of this book is on the character of God, but before we study His *attributes*, we must first understand His *identity* as Father. Therefore, the study of these truths, although they may be reminders to some, are not excursions from our topic but the very foundation without which we cannot proceed.

Enemies, Not Children

If you are a Christian, prior to your conversion you were not a child of God; you were, rather, a child of disobedience (Ephesians 2:2), a child of wrath (Ephesians 2:3), a child of darkness (1 Thessalonians

5:5), an "accursed" child (2 Peter 2:14), and a child of the devil (1 John 3:10). Moreover, you were born, not a citizen of heaven (Philippians 3:20), but an alien to God (Ephesians 2:19) and a resident of "the domain of darkness" (Colossians 1:13). You did not walk in the light (1 John 1:7) but rather "walked according to the course of this world, according to the prince of the power of the air" (Ephesians 2:2). If this language seems like overkill, it's not—it's biblical, and critical to understand, because it's only as we understand our former identity in sin that we can begin to bask in the wonder of our present identity in Christ. Today, many people are quick to pursue the benefits of the gospel without ever understanding their need for the gospel in the first place.

Fundamentals

Growing up as a Chicago native, I had few things cemented in me more than the fact that I was supposed to hate the Green Bay Packers—in my mind, they were the Philistines. But even as a Chicago Bears fan, I have come to love the story that takes place in the summer of 1961 involving the legendary Green Bay Packers coach Vince Lombardi. The 1960 season ended in heartbreak for the Packers—they had blown the lead and lost the NFL Championship Game (now the Super Bowl) in the fourth quarter to the Philadelphia Eagles. On the first day of training camp in 1961, Lombardi's team expected to hear their coach cast the vision for new playbooks, improved strategies, and innovative tactics, but instead Coach Lombardi gathered the whole team, motioned for silence, held up the pigskin, and said, "Gentlemen, this is a football." This is one of the most famous moments in sports history. Lombardi knew that if his team was going to grow, they needed to start with the basics, the fundamentals, such as blocking, tackling, running, throwing, and catching. If they weren't solid on the fundamentals, they would never be solid anywhere else.

Similarly, many professing Christians pursue peace by chasing new methods and modern strategies, yet what they need the most is for someone to say to them, "Ladies and gentlemen, this is the gospel." The fundamentals. The glorious basics of what it means to be a Christian. We can try to find peace and comfort in doing Christian things, reading Christian truths, and meeting with Christian people, but until we are right in regard to the gospel and our standing before God, we will be wrong everywhere else. You cannot build the walls of a house unless the foundation is secure. As Martyn Lloyd-Jones put it, "We have to realize that there are certain things about which we must be perfectly clear before we can ever hope to have peace, and to enjoy the Christian life."[3]

One of the fundamental things we must understand is that, in the Bible, there is a paradoxical relationship between despair and joy—the feeling of the former is fundamental to experiencing the latter. In other words, you will never know true and lasting joy if you have not first despaired of ever trying to earn your way to God. God grants peace only to those who have given up all hope of ever earning their way to Him. Lloyd-Jones called this profound despair the "essential preliminarily to joy."[4]

Growing up in the church, I remember hearing the testimonies of people who were once drug dealers, sex addicts, and ex-convicts and thinking, *I wish a had a radical testimony like that.* In many ways, this type of thinking revealed not only my age but my heart. In desiring a more "marvellous experience" of faith (as Lloyd-Jones put it),[5] I had diminished the miracle that God had done in my heart as a child. There are scores of people who claim Christ today that nod their heads in agreement to the fact that "all have sinned and fall short of the glory of God" (Romans 3:23) but who have never had their mouths shut (Romans 3:19) before a holy God.

When we minimize our former sinful condition, we trivialize the work of Christ, and in doing so we sabotage the joy and peace that the gospel alone can provide. We can sing "Amazing Grace" with our mouths and yet our hearts will never believe grace is amazing until we believe that it "saved a wretch like me." God's grace will never be amazing to those who are not first fully convicted of their sin. *Misery over sin is the prerequisite to joy in Christ.* A diminished view of God produces a diminished view of sin, which leads to a diminished view of grace, which leads to a diminished view of the fatherhood of God and the peace that He alone can provide. You will never know God as Father in an intimate sense until you have first known Him as holy King and righteous Judge. Jesus said that the antidote to anxiety is the consideration of the character of our heavenly Father, but the fatherhood of God is simply a Christian platitude and empty cliché until we come to terms with our sin and come to a healthy fear of God.

Fearing God

What does it mean to fear God? It means to be gripped by His grandeur and glory. It means to put Him in His rightful place. To fear God means that you are in awe of Him, that you worship Him, and that you desire to avoid anything that would dishonor Him. The believer's fear of God as Father is qualitatively different from the fear of God as Judge. But the fear of God as Judge must come before the fear of God as Father. It's when you recognize what Christ has done for you on the cross and come to Him in faith that your fear is transformed. One pastor said, "The gospel is the difference between being afraid of God and fearing God."[6] I like that. Our culture, on a quest to make God more palatable, has all but removed the proper and necessary fear of God. In doing so, all other fears have catapulted back into our lives. Today, many have learned the grace of God before they have learned the fear of God, and as a result they understand neither. There will never be any appreciation of God's grace until you understand His justice, and you will not marvel at the reality of your adoption into the family of God until you consider the alienation you had from Him in your sin. In the hymn "Amazing Grace," the former slave trader penned the line "'Twas grace that taught my heart to fear, and grace my fears relieved; how precious did that grace appear the hour I first believed." Did you catch that? God's grace gives us a proper fear of Him as Father; as a result, all the other fears in life are "relieved"—they are eliminated.

So let me ask you: Have you ever come to the end of yourself? Have you ever come face-to-face with God as a holy King and just Judge? If not, you can cast aside all hopes of knowing the peace only He provides. If you feel the burden of your sin, then you must also know that God cannot forgive sin without punishing it. He does not simply pardon sin in the sense that He dismisses it. He must punish it. So, then, how can God forgive my sin? How can God become my Father? How can God's wrath toward my sin be paid by another? How can I have peace with God so that I might have the peace of God?

Faith and repentance.

By faith we believe in the life, death, and resurrection of Jesus Christ and trust that, on the cross, Jesus took our sins onto Himself and in exchange offers us His righteousness (2 Corinthians 5:21). I've heard it said, "You contribute nothing to your salvation except the sin that made it necessary."[7] This much is true. All we have is sin and all Jesus has is righteousness, and in this great exchange we now by faith are forgiven, cleansed, adopted, and loved. Packer said, "God has taken you from the gutter, so to speak, and made you a son in His house."[8] This monumental love is poured out into our hearts by the power of the Holy Spirit (Romans 5:5), who assures us that we belong to God (Romans 8:16). However familiar this reality may be, we must not allow the familiar to obscure the extraordinary, and we must not pursue novel answers to our anxiety at the expense of concrete ones.

Farewell to Your Past

The path to peace starts with despair. A despair of earning your way to God and then a "farewell once and for all to your past."[9] If you are a Christian, your sin has been paid for, not with perishable things such as silver or gold, "but with precious blood, as of a lamb unblemished and spotless, the blood of Christ" (1 Peter 1:19). Your adoption as a child of God is a free gift to you, but it was costly to God—it cost Him the death of His beloved Son. If you're a Christian, although your sins were as scarlet, they have been washed white as snow in the blood of the Lamb (Isaiah 1:18).

Your past, present, and future sin are forgiven by Jesus Christ.

The path forward begins with a reminder of the fundamentals. We are sinners who deserve judgment, "but God, being rich in mercy, because of His great love with which He loved us, even when we were dead in our wrongdoings, made us alive together with Christ (by grace you have been saved)."[10] God is gracious to save. And He is gracious to transform. You overcome anxiety not by fighting it but by casting it onto Someone greater than you. The pathway to peace starts with knowing God as Father because you have trusted in His Son as Savior. If you have this confidence, then smile—your greatest need in life has already been met. This book is for Christians, so again, it's worth asking, *What is a Christian?* "The richest answer I know is that a Christian is one who has God as Father."[11]

————— Reflection Questions —————

1. Why is grasping the fatherhood of God so important in our Christian life—especially as it relates to anxiety and worry?

2. Read Ephesians 2:1–3. How does the Bible describe our lives before Christ? How might this affect how we think of our lives today? Why is it so important that we do not minimize the miraculous work that God has done in our hearts if we are in Christ? How does a minimization of the gospel relate to our understanding of anxiety?

3. What is the difference between *being afraid of* God and *fearing* God? Where there is little fear of the Lord, there will be little peace. Why do you think that is?

CHAPTER 7

Forever Himself, Forever Good

M y older daughter's name is Lily. Lily Jean Ardavanis. As I'm writing this chapter, she is almost two years old. Lily loves to dance, consumes heaps of strawberries, wears a ladybug costume every day, and sleeps, on average, fourteen hours a night (thank the Lord). We named our daughter Lily because we were drawn to Jesus' teaching on the subject we are examining—how Jesus tells His anxious followers to *consider the lilies*. My wife and I liked the name Lily, and as parents we have the authority to name our child (which is crazy when you think about it). Names stick with you. You carry them and are called *by* them your entire life. What's interesting, however, is that Lily's name (like every other name) was given to her *before* we knew anything about her. What could we possibly know about her idiosyncrasies, personality, disposition, gifts, or temperament while she was still in the womb? Her name doesn't in any way shed light on who she is. Her name is a *title*.

Shakespeare, in his tragic play *Romeo and Juliet*, penned the line: *What's in a name?* The thrust of Juliet's question draws our attention to the arbitrary and irrelevant nature of the titles we possess. Names don't detail our identities and characters. A man named John could be a saint (like John Bunyan) or a mass murderer (like John E. List). But the answer to Juliet's question, "What's in a name?" applies only to *creatures* and differs when we speak of *the Creator*.

In Scripture there are dozens of different names for God, but God's names are not like human names. Why? Because His names are *not* mere titles; they are consummate and representative of His character. Who He is, how He operates, and how He relates to His children are revealed in the names He gives to us in His Word. Furthermore, God's name is not "God." That's His title. His title tells us *what He is*. But God's names tell us *who He is*.

As we have already examined, one of the most precious names for God in Scripture is "Father." If we don't see God as Father, we will have a distorted view of Him. Moreover, if we fail to know God in light of His other *names*, His other *attributes*, then the value and comfort we derive from His fatherly care will be diminished.

In Scripture, God is referred to as the following:

El Shaddai: "The Lord, God Almighty." We see this name
   seven times in Scripture.
Jehovah Jireh: "The LORD will provide." We see this name only
   once, in Genesis 22:14.
El Olam: "The everlasting God." We see this name *four* times
   throughout the Old Testament.
Jehovah Shalom: "The LORD is Peace." We see this name only
   once, in Judges 6:24.

Are you anxious? Are you despairing? Then find comfort in the names of God! Why? Because God's names aren't mere titles—they tell us *who He is* and detail *why* we should trust Him. Interestingly, the most common and most important name for God has, until recently, rarely been translated in true form when we read our English Bibles. These subtle translative decisions have, over time, affected the way we see God.

Diplomats and Deists

The man on the United States one-hundred-dollar bill, Benjamin Franklin, was a deist who had a philosophical and rationalistic view of God and this world. People who adhere to this theological framework do not deny the existence of God altogether; rather, they view God as a clockmaker who wound up the universe and then walked away to become a distant observer and casual spectator of the affairs, events, and history of mankind. To a deist, there is a God, but He is in the stadium of heaven eating popcorn (lightly salted), not interfering, and mindlessly observing the individuals on planet Earth. To a deist, maybe God was active in creation, but now . . . He is retired, His feet are up, and His recliner is reclined. Therefore, don't bother Him. He probably won't hear you, and even if *He did* . . . He wouldn't bother to get involved in any way.

Sadly, many professing Christians view God the same way the deists do: as a distant, impersonal, and retired deity who has little interest and involvement in the affairs of our lives. Consequently, in this view, we have every reason to be anxious! If God is merely a passive observer of our lives, how on earth could we have peace?

Thankfully, of all the names of God, there is one name in particular that melts this type of unbiblical thinking. This name for God isn't used once, twice, or even a hundred times in Scripture—it is used more than 6,800 times. It's the name God revealed to Moses in Exodus 3, and this revelation of God's name is the hammer that shatters the glass of the depersonalized, distant, and consequently paralyzing view of God as merely a "higher power" or an aloof deity. To those who are anxious, knowing God by His name is helpful. Why? Because His title as "God" tells us what He is, but His name tells us *who He is.*

The Far Side of the Wilderness

In Exodus 3, an eighty-year-old shepherd emerges into the spotlight of Scripture. We have met this aged shepherd before, but forty years have passed, and this former prince of Egypt no longer lives in the luxury of Pharaoh's palace but can be found tending his father-in-law's herds in the arid, jagged, and desolate region of Midian. His name, as you likely know, is Moses.

For four decades he had been largely unseen, except by God. And as Moses led his sheep to "the far side of the wilderness" (Exodus 3:1 NIV), he came across something he had never seen: a bush that was burning and yet not consumed (v. 2). The remarkableness of this sight, being extraordinary in and of itself, was compounded when a voice spoke to Moses from the midst of the bush, saying,

> "Moses, Moses!" And he said, "Here I am." Then He said, "Do not come near here; remove your sandals from your feet, for the place on which you are standing is holy ground." (vv. 4–5)

Moses trepidatiously removed his sandals and kept his distance from the One speaking to him. Then God spoke to Moses again, saying,

> "I am the God of your father—the God of Abraham, the God of Isaac, and the God of Jacob." Then Moses hid his face, for he was afraid to look at God. (v. 6)

I expect you may be familiar with how the conversation between God and Moses unfolded. God told Moses that He has seen the affliction of His people and has come down to deliver them (v. 8). How? Through Moses. Moses, the former prince and present shepherd, whose life had been thrust into obscurity for four decades, would now be placed center stage in one of Scripture's most epic stories. Moses's response, however, was not one of eagerness but one of reluctance: "Who am I, that I should go to Pharaoh, and that I should bring the sons of Israel out of Egypt?" (v. 11). God responded by telling Moses that he would not be alone, that God would be with him. Still Moses's uncertainty, fear, and anxiety persisted at the prospect of his duel with Pharaoh, the most powerful man on earth. Moses again asked: "Behold, I am going to the sons of Israel, and I will say to them, 'The God of your fathers has sent me to you.' Now they may say to me, 'What is His name?' What shall I say to them?" (v. 13).

Moses was anxious. He was fearful. How could he take on the armies of Pharaoh? Amid his understandable fear, his most pressing question for the One speaking to Him was, interestingly, *What is Your name?* In Exodus 3:14–15, God responded to Moses's question, and in doing so He revealed not only His name but His nature—*who He is.*

> God said to Moses, "I AM WHO I AM"; and He said, "Thus you shall say to the sons of Israel, 'I AM has sent me to you.' . . . Thus you shall say to the sons of Israel, 'The LORD [YHWH], the God of your fathers, the God of Abraham, the God of Isaac, and the God of Jacob, has sent me to you.' This is My name forever, and this is My memorial name to all generations."

YAHWEH

God responded to Moses by saying *ehyeh asher ehyeh*, which is translated "I AM WHO I AM" or "I WILL BE WHAT I WILL BE."

Then God told Moses to tell the children of Israel, "I AM has sent me to you" (Exodus 3:14). Again, God's name is not "God"; that's His title. His name, as He revealed Himself to Moses, is "I AM WHO I AM."

If you were to ask me "Who are you?" and I responded, "I am who I am," that would be true, but it may not be the answer you were looking for. It may seem to be stating the obvious. Of course I am who I am. If I gave this answer to you, it may even seem as though I was eluding your question altogether, attempting to conceal my identity. But that wasn't the case for God when He spoke of Himself to Moses. He was not hiding Himself; He was disclosing who He is.

The names "I AM" and "Yahweh" are both derived from the same Hebrew word *hiyah*, which is the verb "to be." The difference between these words is simple: *Ehyeh* ("I AM") is in the first person, and *YHWH* ("Yahweh") is in the third person, meaning, "He is." For centuries, the Jewish people were so afraid of taking God's name in vain (in observance of the third commandment) that they would seldom, if ever, utter the name from their lips. Because of this, when they addressed *YHWH*, they pronounced it *Adonai*, which means "my Lord." For many years, the English translations have followed suit and routinely translate the name *YHWH* as "LORD." But something personal, precious, and comforting is missed when we translate *YHWH* as "LORD" or when we simply refer to God as "God." That would be like referring to my spouse as "person" instead of as "Caity Jean."

Furthermore, it's one thing to believe *in* God, but it's an entirely different thing to believe God and know Him by His personal name. Sadly, many professing Christians believe in God in the same way they believe in oxygen. They believe He *exists*, but that belief has little to do with how they live their lives. Their view of God is very similar to that of a deist. As we will observe, God's name alone is the most powerful implication of His existence. His name means "I AM," and in a world that is grasping to know whether He is truly there, the third-person rendering of God's name gives us the answer: "He is."

God gave His personal name to Moses because trust in God is rooted foremost not in what He has done or what He can do but in *who He is*. John Calvin once said we can never know who we are until we know who God is.[1] Moses asked the question: "Who are you?" And God responded by saying: "I AM." Is this cryptic or is this powerful? Well, let's go back to Shakespeare's question, *What's in a name?* If God's name simply means "He is," then what exactly *is* God? At the time Moses encountered Yahweh at the burning bush, the Hebrews were languishing under the oppression of their Egyptian taskmasters; they had been slaves for four hundred years, and their future looked bleak. And Moses, the one assigned to deliver them, needed to know that God didn't merely *exist* but that God was knowable, present, and sufficient to deliver them. The name of God might seem like an interesting topic to bring up in a book on anxiety, fear, and despair, but this is one of the principal grounds in which your faith must be rooted. As we survey the declarations that God made about His covenant name, and their implications, we will examine three essential truths that function as the necessary sustenance for our oft-feeble faith.

1. Yahweh Is Self-Existent

When I was a camp director, one of my favorite traditions we had was to light a big bonfire every Friday evening before the campers returned home (this tradition has been going on for decades and is still going strong!). The fire would bring warmth and light to the one thousand teenage students gathered in the large outdoor amphitheater, and as with building any fire, a few preliminary steps were necessary: wood must be gathered, gasoline must be poured, and a match must be struck. Instantly, the wood would be ablaze, the flames would soar high into the air, and the oohs and aahs of the students would echo through the forest.

Anyone who has been to a campfire understands this basic reality: fires need to be started. The stovetop fire and the forest fire alike both begin with a tiny spark. They are dependent on external causation.

But in the stunning encounter between God and Moses at the burning bush, God Himself and the fire within the bush bear striking similarity: both are uncaused. The fire in the bush was not started by an external agent; it was self-generated and self-existent. How? Because the self-existent God was in the bush. Ironically, even though the scene we are examining with God and Moses in the Midianite desert is referred to as "the burning bush," the truth is the bush wasn't *burning* at all. The passage says that the "bush was burning with fire, yet the bush was not consumed" (Exodus 3:2). The imagery of the bush and the nature of the fire goes to show us something about the essence of God.

As Yahweh revealed Himself to Moses as the "I AM," we are reminded that one of the core tenets of God's character is that He and He alone is the sole cause of everything in creation and that He Himself has no original cause. God is not the one who "once was" or the God who will one day "become." He is the God who *is* and is, therefore, the I AM. Our faith will rise only as high as our perception of God's character. And one of the things we must understand about God is that when we go to Him in prayer, we go to a God who has no "potential." Everything in our lives and in this world is in a state of flux—situations, circumstances, and people around us are changing. But God . . . He is not *becoming*; He simply *is*. The theological term *aseity* is employed to convey God's self-existence and is derived from the Latin term *a*, which means "from," and *se*, which means "self." Therefore, God's aseity means that He derives life in and of Himself and His existence is owed to nothing and no one.

Maybe this sounds a bit heady for a book focused on anxiety and despair, but worship and trust can begin only when we understand that the God on whom we cast all our cares is fundamentally distinct from us in this matter. People, planets, and products all have a cause for their existence, but God, and God alone, exists by His own power. Fires come from sparks, trees come from seeds, and people come from their biological parents, but God has no primary cause outside of Himself—He is self-existent, and because He is, He is also the only One capable of being our Creator.

Anxiety is inevitable in a world that teaches us that human beings are grown-up goo, clumps of cells, and the products of a big bang. If our entire existence is the result of unseen forces, cosmic accidents, and chance, what's to prevent our lives (and the life of our planet, for that matter) from being thrown into a further tailspin? The indoctrination of evolution over the past century has not only crippled our sense of human dignity as God's image bearers but also created the perception of a universe where everything is held together by chance and sheer luck.

If you were to ask the question "Who made God?" what would be the answer? No one—no one made God. Why is that special? Because it's only in coming to grips with that reality can we then ask the question I ask my daughter Lily: "Who made you?" To which she replies: "God." Sometimes the most fundamental truths are the ones most suppressed, ignored, or attacked. I will discuss this in greater detail soon, but for now you need to understand that only a self-existent God can create you. You are not the product of chance but the image bearer of the only self-existent God. Because God is the "I AM," He has no potential and will not and cannot be a better God in the future than He is right now and has been for all of eternity past.

2. Yahweh Is Self-Sufficient

As you can imagine, once the great campfire was started, it needed to be *sustained*. Unless additional fuel was added to the fire, the fire would die. Like fires, all people, planets, plants, and products have a cause, but not only that—all of them need to be sustained in order to survive. Planets need gravity, trees need water, products need batteries, and people (like this guy) need food (preferably fried eggs). Because our God is self-existent, however, He alone is also *self-sufficient* (Acts 17:25). This is huge. As you read this book, you may be faint and weary, anxiety may seem overwhelming, fear may be invading the depths of your mind, but Scripture compels us to cast our cares onto a God who is "the Everlasting God, the LORD, the Creator of the ends of the earth," and He "does not become weary or tired" (Isaiah 40:28). Christians affirm the power of God, but God's power is unique in this way: *He never needs to recharge.* God has no backup generator that keeps the solar system spinning in case He is drained by world events. He plugs into no external source of power, but everything in all of creation plugs into the power that He provides as the self-existent and self-sufficient One (Hebrews 1:3).

Are you anxious? Then cast all your needs onto the God who has none.

Do you need to be sustained amid life's trials? Then come to the Everlasting Refuge who needs no sustaining at all.

God isn't simultaneously meeting His own needs as He attends to ours. When we come to Him in prayer, we aren't bothering a busy God who is scrambling to survive, we are speaking to a God who is not "served by human hands, as though He needed anything, since He Himself gives to all people life and breath and all things" (Acts 17:24–25). Left to ourselves, we have many needs, but because our Shepherd has none, we can say with the psalmist: "The LORD is my shepherd; I shall not want" (Psalm 23:1 NKJV).

3. Yahweh Is Eternal

As Moses approached the burning bush, Yahweh introduced Himself as "the God of your father, the God of Abraham, the God of Isaac, and the God of Jacob" (Exodus 3:6). Moses's first encounter with Yahweh began with the understanding of a critical truth about Him: Yahweh is the only self-existent, self-sufficient, and *eternal* God. Interestingly, this conviction regarding God's eternality is not only what marked the beginning of Moses's ministry but also that which girded Moses with strength until the very end. Forty years after this encounter with God, Moses was no longer the shepherd of sheep but the shepherd of the Hebrew people. En route to the promised land, Moses, the pastor of two million people, witnessed an entire generation die and conducted more funeral services than anyone else in history. During his four decades in the wilderness, Moses was constantly reminded of the transience and fragility of life. It's against this backdrop of life's brevity that Moses wrote the first psalm ever written and the only one ascribed to him. In Psalm 90, Moses said, "Lord, You have been our dwelling place in all generations. Before the mountains were born or You gave birth to the earth and the world, even from everlasting to everlasting, You are God" (vv. 1–2).

My former cabin in the woods was situated near a beautiful lake. Although surrounded by the snowcapped peaks of the Sierras, the water was warm in the summer (perfect for paddleboarding). I used to tease kids by asking them, "Hey, who do you think made this lake?" They would pause for a moment and then respond, "God?" And then I would joke and say, "No . . . John made that lake." To which they would reply, "Huh?"

It's true.

The eighty-seven-acre lake lies behind the world's first concrete-reinforced multiple-arch dam, designed by John S. Eastwood and constructed in 1908 by the Hume-Bennett Lumber Company.

Originally, the man-made lake was used as a flume to transport cut lumber down to Sanger, California. Although engineered and constructed by men, the lake itself is nevertheless beautiful. The mountains that surround the lake, however, were not made by John Eastwood, the builder of arched dams; those picturesque peaks were begotten by God. Before the United States was founded and before your grandpa's grandpa was born, those mountains were there.

In the Bible, the mountains are symbols of solidity and strength; they draw our attention upward and cause us to consider this reality articulated by Moses: "Before the mountains were born or You gave birth to the earth and the world, even from everlasting to everlasting, You are God" (Psalm 90:2). Moses was reflecting. The wilderness he wandered was a sea of tombstones—and as he considered the brevity of life, he looked up to the mountains and thought, *Although these mountains are ancient to me, they are babes to God. He and He alone is from everlasting to everlasting.* In Psalm 90:4, Moses was still meditating on God's eternality and said: "For a thousand years in Your sight are like yesterday when it passes by, or as a watch in the night." The empires of the previous millennium are mere blinks on the scale of God's eternality. The lengthiest stretches of time, even thousands or millions of years, are merely baby blips on the radar to our eternal God.

You and I *became.* Our lives had a beginning, right now we are in a state of *becoming,* and one day our lives will have an end. Sinclair Ferguson put it this way: "We became, we are becoming, and we were."[2] But not God. He had no *beginning,* He is not *becoming,* and He will not end; He simply is the eternal I AM. The depth of these thoughts is enough to cause our minds to implode, yet we must pray that God would give us the grace to comprehend them.

You may be asking, *What does God's eternality have to do with my anxiety?*

Well, to Moses, a lot. Forty years earlier, Moses had stood before

God and had been given the daunting task of delivering the Israelite people from the hand of Pharaoh. His fear and anxiety over his disability and over the task itself caused an internal panic: *Who am I that I could do this?* And yet here is when God began to comfort and encourage Moses: "I, and I alone, am the everlasting God." At times, the truth of God's eternality may be so familiar to our minds that it may just slip off the tip of our tongues. But God wanted Moses to know something in the moment of his greatest fear: "Pharaoh has a beginning and an end, but only I am from everlasting to everlasting." Whatever battle you may be facing in your life, put it against the backdrop of our eternal God who disposes of kings, kingdoms, and empires without batting an eye. If you feel out of place, like a tumbleweed bouncing around the wilderness floor—then find comfort in the fact that God is not only eternal, but He is our "dwelling place in all generations" (Psalm 90:1). Generations come, generations go, but one thing stays the same: God's commitment to be His people's eternal home.

The hymn writer Isaac Watts, reflecting on the words of Moses, penned the following words in the early eighteenth century:

> O God, our Help in ages past,
> our Hope for years to come,
> our Shelter from the stormy blast,
> and our eternal Home.

Knowing God by Name

In considering the covenant name of God, we are forced to contemplate His essence. God's name is I AM. This means all that He is, He has been, and all He has been He will be. This truth is simple enough for a child to bathe in and yet deep enough for an elephant to swim.³ God's name means that He and He alone is the self-existent, self-sufficient, and eternal God. His name, Yahweh, reminds us that we are creatures, He is the Creator, we have many needs, He has none, we are transient, He is forever. Remember how we defined faith? Faith is gazing at God. And for the one who seeks to deepen and develop their gaze, this is the foot of the mountain: your Father is the I AM. Confoundingly, the One who never had a beginning, never is becoming, and will never have an end is also the One who told Moses, "I have surely seen the oppression of My people . . . and have heard their cry" (Exodus 3:7 NKJV).

What is profoundly humbling is this: our self-existent, self-sufficient, and eternal God is not a passive observer of the affairs and sufferings of His people; He sees our affliction and hears our cries. As we will observe in greater detail in the next chapter, the immensity of God's essence does not create distance between Him and those who belong to Him. Astonishingly, it is in His eternal immensity that we experience the intimacy and security our hearts long for.

Reflection Questions

1. Why are God's names different from titles? What do His names tell us about His nature?

2. What are areas of your life in which you try to be self-sufficient? What reminds you that you are not? How can God's nature reframe how we think about our worries? How does a small view of God's power diminish our ability to trust Him?

3. How can the eternal nature of God be a comfort to you? Think beyond the theologically "correct" answer and consider this question personally for *you*.

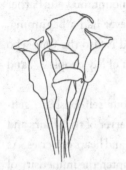

CHAPTER 8

Infinite Understanding

LORD, *You have searched me and known me.*
PSALM 139:1

Anxiety isolates us.
Worry detaches us.
Depression disconnects us from those we love.
Why? Because vulnerability in relationships is dependent on transparency—on being known. And when we feel as if no one understands the pain we endure or grasps the worries we face, we often withdraw. The other side of the "misery loves company" coin is that misery *hates* company. If no one understands me or comprehends my pain, why would I spend time with anyone? How can I connect with others when they are oblivious to the anxiety in my mind and to the pain within my heart? Their anxious lament is this:

If only there was someone who "gets me." If only there was someone who understands me. If only I could be fully and truly known.

Alternatively, the prospect of being fully known may be the very thing that prompts our anxiety in the first place. The lives we live are often shrouded in posturing and performing. As a result, there is a looming fear that if people knew the *real me*—that is, the me behind my facades—then they would no longer desire to know me at all. Therefore, masquerades bring safety, and exposure brings anxiety. Our anxious fear is that, one day, *the real me will be exposed*, and when I am known, *I will not be loved.*

Thus, for some, the feeling of being unknown fuels anxiety, while, for others, being unknown is the only source of comfort. In both cases, the question is this: What does God say in His Word? How does our heavenly Father comfort, encourage, and correct people like us who feel this way? In what way does He know His children? To answer that, we must turn to the Psalms, where we find the balming and captivating truth of God's omniscience.

Your Father Knows

The word *omniscience* is derived from two Latin words—*omnus*, meaning "all," and *scientia*, meaning "knowledge." Therefore, God's omniscience means He is *all knowing*. You may be so familiar with this idea that you've become apathetic to its truth. So pause here, if need be, and pray that God's Spirit will soften your callous and indifferent heart to this momentous truth that provides unspeakable comfort for the anxious and worried.

God's omniscience means He knows everything. And everything He knows He knows exhaustively. Therefore, God knows no one thing and no one person better than another; He knows all things, people, and places equally well. God's knowledge is unquantifiable and immeasurable (Psalm 147:5). And His knowledge is fundamentally different from the knowledge you or I can possess. Let me explain why.

In order for me to do anything, such as cook an egg, tie my shoes, shoot a basketball, balance a budget, and so forth, I first had to learn how to do it. All human apprehension is based on acquisition—everything you know is something that you have acquired, or *learned*. But God's knowledge is not derived; it's not acquired or learned. It's inherent to who He is. Remember, God is the I AM, which means He is not in a state of developing—He is not a supercomputer equipped with AI that makes split-second calculations and decisions and grows stronger with age.

He *already* knows.

Everything.

While it may be true for us that we learn something new every day, it's not true for God. He is *omniscient*.

What God Isn't Like

Sometimes when we come to the study of God's character, it is easier to describe what God is *not* like so that we can understand what He *is* like. For example, the apostle Paul said that God cannot lie (Titus 1:2), against the backdrop of man's lies and deception. Elsewhere, the Bible states that, with God, nothing is impossible (Luke 1:37), which is contrasted by the inability of human beings. In that same vein, this is what our heavenly Father's omniscience means:

He never counts.
He never discovers.
He is never surprised.
He is never amazed (except at Himself).

He never wonders.

He never learns.

He never remembers (because He never forgets).

He is never reminded.

He never understands more clearly.

He never misinterprets.

He is never made aware, and He never receives counsel.

In the book of Job, Job asked: "Can anyone teach God knowledge?" (21:22).

Answer: No.

Isaiah asked the question: "Who has directed the Spirit of the LORD, or as His counselor has informed Him? With whom did He consult and who gave Him understanding? And who taught Him in the path of justice and taught Him knowledge?" (Isaiah 40:13–14).

What's the answer? Who counseled God?

No one.

Who informed God?

No one.

Who gave God understanding?

No one.

If God were to learn, that would be a violation of His immutability (His changelessness). But God says, "I, the LORD, do not change" (Malachi 3:6). The I AM does not change and, therefore, cannot learn.

You may be asking, *What does this have to do with my anxiety?*

Well, remember, Jesus urged the anxious to consider the character of their heavenly Father. Jesus did not simply provide "five steps to annihilate anxiety"; instead, He provided an exalted view of our Father. In coming to a deeper understanding of God's character, we are relieved, as A. W. Tozer said, of "ten thousand temporal problems."[1]

Maybe you have asked, "How much does my heavenly Father know me? Does He know my pain? Does He know the future? Does He know my past? Does He know my sin? Does He love the real me or the postured version that I present to others?" All of these questions find their biblical answers in the lofty doctrine of God's omniscience.

The Immensity of God's Omniscience

God's knowledge of us is tremendously intimate, and yet, to be struck by the intimacy of His knowledge, we must first come to grips with the immensity of God's knowledge.

God's Knowledge of Nature

Space.com roughly estimates that there are ten trillion galaxies in the universe. And in our galaxy, the Milky Way, there are an estimated one hundred billion stars alone. Therefore, if you were to multiply the number of stars within one galaxy by the total number of galaxies within the universe, you would arrive at an unfathomable number: 1,000,000,000,000,000,000,000,000 stars ("1 septillion in the American numbering system").[2] And yet Psalm 147:4 reads, "He determines the number of the stars; he gives to all of them their names" (ESV). The night sky hosts a great multitude of stars, some that dazzle, some that die, many that remain unknown and undiscovered by man—yet not one of them is unknown or unnamed by God. He knows them all.

Stars are indeed big and shiny, but God is no more aware of the sun than He is of the animal that is small and fluffy. The BBC estimates that there are nearly 1,918,000 baby rabbits born every day in the UK alone.[3] And do you know what? God knows the moment and the location of every single bunny's birth. In the book of Job, God was silent for thirty-seven chapters while Job and his friends pontificated about why Job's life was falling apart. And when God responded, He not only proclaimed His sovereignty, but He broadcast His omniscience. God asked Job, "Is it by your understanding that the hawk soars?" (Job 39:26). "Do you help goats give birth?" (Job 39:1, author paraphrase). God is so comprehensive in His knowledge that He functions as the midwife to the most distant goat on the most distant mountain. God said to Job, *I am a parent to my universe. The snow leopards in the Himalayas, the smallest fish in the deepest ocean trench, the lion in the savanna, the hawk that soars, the stars in the sky . . . they answer to Me, and I know them all.* Jesus conveyed the breathtaking nature of God's omniscience in Matthew 10:29–30: "Are not two sparrows sold for a penny? And not one of them will fall to the ground apart from your Father. But even the hairs of your head are all numbered" (ESV).

God's Knowledge of Nations

Not only is God's knowledge of nature exhaustive, so is His knowledge of nations. The Joshua Project estimates that there are 17,313 people groups in the world.[4] That is 17,313 people groups that possess ethnic and linguistic distinctions. Astoundingly, God knows the happenings, the doings, and the rulings of all of them simultaneously with a perfect, complete, and exhaustive knowledge. He not only knows the rulers of these nations; He knows the individuals within them.

God is no more aware of Joe Biden than He is of Joe Schmo.

He is no more attentive to Prince Harry than He is to the everyday Tom, Dick, and Harry.

He is no more cognizant of chief executive officers than He is of the tribal chiefs in the remotest jungles.

As I was studying the doctrine of God's omniscience, I read

that God's omniscience is often left unattended because it's hard to apply. You may be wondering, *What does this have to do with worry? Okay, I get it. God knows everything. He has a full, complete, perfect, and exhaustive understanding of Himself, of nature, and of nations. He names every star and every sparrow, and He knows every drop of rain. So what?*

Well, first of all, it is the Christian's highest privilege and joy to know what our God and Creator is like. And second, the attribute of God's omniscience is wonderful, not only because it reveals the *immensity* of God's knowledge, but also because it reveals the *intimacy* in which He knows you if you are one of His children.

The Intimacy of God's Omniscience

As David contemplated the truth of God's omniscience in Psalm 139, he did so not as an academic exercise but as a soul-satisfying, anxiety-exploding, and heart-thrilling meditation. Like many of us, David experienced prolonged seasons of loneliness and isolation. David cried out to God in Psalm 25:16: "Turn to me and be gracious to me, for I am lonely and afflicted." In other seasons of his life, David experienced the worry of being fully known after he committed both adultery and murder. The man who longed to be known when he resided in caves feared to be fully known when he resided in the palace. In both cases and in both places, God's omniscience would bring David comfort.

Let's briefly consider the passage in Scripture that most clearly displays the all-encompassing knowledge of God. Psalm 139 is one of my favorite psalms, and it's David's magnum opus on God's omniscience. In this psalm, David reflects on the reality that the God who knows all people, all planets, and all matters also intimately and personally knows you.

God Knows You

David begins Psalm 139 by saying, "LORD, You have searched me and known me" (v. 1). The same Hebrew word for "search" is used when Joshua and Caleb went to "spy out" the promised land. It involves much more than a mere casual glance; it describes the fact that God investigates and inspects our hearts. He leaves no stone unturned. Every hidden nook and cranny of our hearts is fully known by Him. Even that which may be unseen on the surface is dug up and explored by the great archaeologist and excavator of our hearts. David said that God had searched and *known* him. In considering God's omniscience, we are tempted to interpret God's knowledge as *awareness*, but the Hebrew word for "know" that David employed here is *yada*, which is the same word used to describe Adam's intimate relationship with Eve in Genesis. In Psalm 8, David is looking up at the stars (like many of us do) and is baffled and blown away as he asks God, "What is man that you are mindful of him?" (v. 4 ESV). Yet David details in Psalm 139 that God is not merely "mindful" of His children; He *knows* them.

Deeply.

Personally.

Exhaustively.

God doesn't just know you exist; He doesn't just know your name; He doesn't just occasionally check in on you. He knows every hair on your head (Matthew 10:30) and every recess within your heart (Jeremiah 17:10). Augustine (354–430) once acknowledged that though he had become a great puzzle to himself,[5] God speaks to His despairing children through His Word, "You are not a puzzle nor a mystery to me. I know you." This is a staggering, humbling, and comforting truth. The God who knows a million things at once, billions of galaxies, 17,313 people groups has set His mind on you and knows you deeply. So much so that while you read this chapter, you are looked at and known by God as if there was not another creature in creation but yourself.

God Knows Your Actions

David says in Psalm 139:2–3 that God knows when we sit down and when we rise up. In Hebrew literature these opposites of "sitting" and "rising" are called a merism, which is a literary device that takes two actions on opposite sides of the spectrum and includes everything in between. For example, Genesis 1:1 reads, "In the beginning God created the heavens and the earth." But not only did God create the heavens and the earth, He created everything in between. Therefore, David is not simply saying that God gets punch cards of our day each morning and evening, but that our every moment and action is known by God.

You have never done a single thing, gone to a single place, or experienced any event that is unknown to God.

God Knows Your Heart

When God sent the prophet Samuel to anoint a new king over Israel, seemingly qualified and capable sons of Jesse were overlooked. But God spoke these familiar words to Samuel amid his search for a new king: "God sees not as man sees, for man looks at the outward appearance, but the LORD looks at the heart" (1 Samuel 16:7). Years later, the same anointed king would pen these words, "Even before there is a word on my tongue, behold, LORD, You know it all" (Psalm 139:4). Our lips are a window into our hearts (Matthew 12:34), but God doesn't need to hear us speak to see into our hearts. Even unspoken words from our lips are known by the God who searches and knows our hearts. This might terrify those who are running from God, but David rejoiced over these realities. David knew that when he went to God in prayer, he did not need to fear being misunderstood by God, and he did not need to fear being overlooked by

God, despite the great throngs who come to God with their petitions and their needs. God knows our hearts. When David's stammering tongue could not say what he wished to say, he resigned everything unto His heavenly Father and said, "Lord, you know . . . you know."

Have you thought about this? That your heart, disposition, thoughts, and personality are known by God?

God Knows Your Needs

David continues, "You hem me in behind and before, and you lay your hand upon me" (Psalm 139:5 NIV). God has hemmed in, or enveloped, His children so closely that there is not a single thing they need that He is not intimately aware of. Furthermore, David says, "You lay your hand upon me." This is God's hand of protection, provision, and fatherly care. Even if you may be walking through deep valleys and dark storms, God's guiding hand is on your life, and He promises to meet your needs. Paul said in Philippians 4:19, "My God will supply all your needs according to His riches in glory in Christ Jesus." Interestingly, Paul wrote these words not from a country club but from a prison cell and yet he still confidently stated that God will meet all our needs.

If you are concerned about your financial, relational, familial, and personal needs, the truth of Scripture is "your Father knows what you need before you ask Him" (Matthew 6:8). We have so many needs that arise, yet Jesus tells us that our omniscient Father already knows each and every single one of them (Matthew 6:32). For this reason, Jesus said, "Do not worry about tomorrow" (Matthew 6:34). All our needs are known and numbered by our good Father who cares more about our needs than we do. Augustine said, "God is more anxious to bestow his blessings on us than we are to receive them."[6] We do not have a Father who is indifferent to our needs; we have a Father who knows them and promises to meet our every need in Christ Jesus (Philippians 4:19).

God Knows You in the Dark

When I lived in the mountains, at times it was so dark I couldn't see my hand in front of my face. And yet David's anxious soul knew this: "If I say, 'Surely the darkness will overwhelm me, and the light around me will be night,' even the darkness is not dark to You, and the night is as bright as the day. Darkness and light are alike to You" (Psalm 139:11–12). These lines that David wrote speak to the reality of God's omnipresence (He is everywhere), but only in relation to explaining His omniscience. The reason God knows everything in every place is that He Himself is everywhere. David finds great comfort in the truth that there is nowhere in the world where you are not under the omniscient gaze of God. God knows you in every place, not because He follows you there, but because He is *already* there.

Not only does God know as we walk through dark places but also as we walk through dark seasons. There is a heart cry that accompanies those who are going through dark days. *If only someone could grasp my pain.* The truth of God's omniscience details that there is no area of your life where God cannot say, "My child, though no one else in the world knows, I know. I know exactly what you are passing through." David said, "Even there your hand will guide me" (Psalm 139:10 NIV). In unfamiliar, strange, dark, and painful places, the all-knowing and all-present hand of God comes to guide those who suffer. The clouds are no canopy, and the night is no curtain to prevent our Father from seeing and knowing His children. For this reason, Hagar, in her loneliest moment, referred to God as *El Roi*, which is pregnant with meaning. *El* means "God," and *Roi* means "to see." Hagar said, "You are a God who sees" (Genesis 16:13).

And indeed He does. He sees all our pain, all our trouble, all our affliction. When we walk in the dark and when tears fall down our faces, the testimony of Scripture is that God catches every falling tear in His bottle and He writes them down in his book (Psalm 56:8).

God Knows Your Frame

Do you struggle with your identity? Then think about this: God knew you when you were one of fifteen possible names in your parent's mind. All children, even the unplanned, unexpected, and unwanted are known and knit together by our omniscient God. David writes these words:

> For You formed my inward parts;
> You covered me in my mother's womb.
> I will praise You, for I am fearfully and wonderfully
>   made.
> Marvelous are Your works,
> And that my soul knows very well.
> My frame was not hidden from You,
> When I was made in secret,
> And skillfully wrought in the lowest parts of the
>   earth." (Psalm 139:13–15 NKJV)

Although there are billions of cells within a tiny fetus, each and every one of those cells is known by God as the Weaver of every life. Deists believe that God created a process whereby life could continue without Him, but Scripture informs us that we are not merely the products of a sexual union between two people but the "workmanship" of a loving, intentional, and all-knowing Creator (Ephesians 2:10).

As individuals, we are often broken, confused, and bent. We need someone who understands us. God "gets" you. He made you in the womb. Your genetic constitution and your embryonic existence were woven by the divine Weaver. He knew you then; therefore, He must know you now. And because of this, you're not a statistic to God. He loves, cares, and knows that which He has made. Psalm 103:14 says that our heavenly Father "knows our frame" (NKJV), which means that your disposition, temperament, countenance, and physical constitution are not only known by God and created by God but loved by Him as well. David is thrust toward thankfulness when He considers that God's knowledge of him didn't begin when he became king, nor even when he was a shepherd boy, but rather when he was a fetus in his mother's womb. For this reason, David says, "I will praise You, for I am fearfully and wonderfully made" (Psalm 139:14 NKJV).

God Knows Your Days

David said in Psalm 139:16, "All the days ordained for me were written in your book before one of them came to be" (NIV). Our lifespans are sovereignly determined and omnisciently known by God. Recently, my wife and I welcomed our second daughter. She was born three weeks earlier than her due date, but not a moment earlier than God had planned. From the cradle to the grave and every day in between, God knows. Your birthday, your death day, and when "it's just been one of *those* days." He knows.

God Knows Best

God not only knows our actions, our hearts, our frame, and our days, He also *knows best*—He is infinite in His wisdom. You could possess all the knowledge in the world and still be a fool, because intelligence does not always equate to wisdom. But God's knowledge is always conjoined to His wisdom. They are two sides of the same coin. At times in our own lives, we may have all the right information but not be sure which direction or path to take, but God never is grasping at straws in discerning what to do with what He knows. He knows what to do with His perfect knowledge because He is also infinite in His wisdom. Paul contemplated this profound truth and was compelled to burst forth into praise: "Oh, the depth of the *riches, both of the wisdom and knowledge* of God! How unsearchable are His judgments and unfathomable His ways!" (Romans 11:33, emphasis added).

Man's Response to God's Omniscience

How should we respond to our Father's omniscience? Much could be said here, but I want to summarize four responses to the truth of God's omniscience.

DOXOLOGY: David said, "Such knowledge is too wonderful for me, too lofty for me to attain" (Psalm 139:6 NIV). All great truths about God should result in great worship to Him. Think about it—the God who knows us better than anyone else and better than we know ourselves is also the One who loves us the most. If you're a Christian, no skeleton is going to come out of the closet that will turn the heart of God away. J. I. Packer said it best:

> What matters supremely, therefore, is not, in the last analysis, the fact that I know God, but the larger fact which underlies it—the fact that he knows me. I am graven on the palms of his hands. I am never out of his mind. All my knowledge of him depends on his sustained initiative in knowing me. I know him because he first knew me, and continues to know me. He knows me as a friend, one who loves me; and there is no moment when his eye is off me, or his attention distracted from me, and no moment therefore, when his care falters. . . . There is tremendous relief in knowing that

his love to me is utterly realistic, based on every point on prior knowledge of the worst about me, so that no discovery now can disillusion him from me, in the way I am so often disillusioned about myself, and quench his determination to bless me.[7]

SECURITY: David said, "When I awake, I am still with You" (Psalm 139:18). The knowledge of God's knowledge of us is the truest security blanket for the Father's children. While you sleep, your Father watches over you, and when you rise, He is there right beside you. It's our knowledge of God's knowledge of us that gives us a place to stand amid life's changing and swirling landscapes. Our lives are full of instability, but amid the chaos we are hemmed in behind and before by the God who knows us and guides us (v. 5).

FREEDOM: As we see in the story of Job, God's omniscience frees us from trying to be God. It frees me to be a creature and let him be the Creator. It allows me to walk in the unknown because my heavenly Father already knows all things. We can "lean not on [our] own understanding" (Proverbs 3:5 NKJV) only because God's understanding is infinite (Psalm 147:5). Furthermore, God's omniscience frees me from trying to be someone or something I'm not. If God knows me, made me, and searches the nooks and crannies of my heart and still extends His love toward me, *why would I pretend to be someone else?* This, of course, is not saying we justify any ungodly sin, but that our natural appearance, personality, gifting, and so forth is completely known by God.

TRUST: Our lives are often shrouded in darkness. There are times we walk in the dark, and yet we know that our omniscient

God is going to one day bring clarity out of the confusion and shed light into the darkness.

Does God Know You?

We have just examined God's profound and perfect knowledge of all things. Yet a careful distinction must be made. God's intimate knowledge of individuals is reserved for those who have placed their faith in His Son Jesus Christ. When Scripture speaks of God's "knowledge," it is a redemptive word. It means more than awareness, it means relationship. It is a knowledge that implies personal affection, redeeming action, faithfulness, and providential watchfulness toward those whom the Father has adopted. Jesus said that there will be some who stand before God at the judgment and hear "*I never knew you*; depart from me" (Matthew 7:23 ESV, emphasis added). Of course God knows them, but not in an intimate and salvific way. Jesus said in John 10:14, "I am the good shepherd, and *I know My own* and My own know Me" (emphasis added). The truth of God's infinite knowledge is only comforting to those who are *known by God*. And the only way to be known by the Father is to come in faith to His only beloved Son. If you're a Christian, this is the pillow you can lay your head on at night: "I am known by God."

———————— Reflection Questions ————————

1. Have you ever thought about the fact that the One who knows you the best (and consequently knows you at your worst) is the One who loves you the most? What does this tell you about your Father's love if you are His child?

2. Read Psalm 139. How does the immensity of God's knowledge lead you to a greater appreciation of the intimacy with which He knows you? How does the realization of God's knowledge of your every thought, action, and difficulty produce doxology, security, freedom, and trust?

3. The overlooked and rejected Hagar called God an amazing name: *El Roi*. Why? Because "You are a God who sees me" (Genesis 16:13). We often feel unseen. How can you personally connect, like Hagar, to the incredible reality of being seen by God?

CHAPTER 9

Above All

O ne of the most printed and most translated English books of all time is *The Pilgrim's Progress*. The beloved story has sold hundreds of millions of copies, been translated into over 200 languages, and, other than the Bible itself, has influenced more diverse readers and writers than any other book. Authors such as John Steinbeck, Charles Dickens, Mark Twain, and C. S. Lewis all refer to this fascinating story and captivating tale that the preacher, John Bunyan, wrote in the late seventeenth century.

In this classic book, Bunyan allegorizes the Christian life and masterfully illustrates the heartbreaks, temptations, snares, troubles, and hostilities that the follower of Jesus endures. The story details the journey of a man, appropriately named Christian, who is traveling from the City of Destruction (this present world) to the Celestial City (heaven), and throughout the book the reader encounters soldiers, dragons, giants, castles, valleys, cities, Vanity Fair, and a man who is weighed down by a great burden upon his back.

I'll never forget reading the book for the first time as a boy—the characters and the plot grabbed me then and its truth and depth continue to shape me now. Each time I reread the book, new morsels of biblical truth affect me, and I'm always struck by the fact that even though Bunyan's story is riddled with imaginative creatures and characters, the story is cherished because every creature, character, and location represents someone, someplace, or something that is very *real* to the reader. For example, on Christian's journey to the Celestial City, he falls into the Slough of *Despond*, is later imprisoned by Giant *Despair*, and then is badly beaten in *Doubting* Castle. Despondency is when our hope and vitality are but a mere flicker; despair is when that flicker has all been snuffed out; and doubt is when we lose sight of (or fail to believe in) our Father's love, goodness, wisdom, and power—do you know the feeling? On Christian's journey, the confluence of despondency, despair, and doubt escalate greater degrees of anxiety and pain in Christian's mind and heart.

I used to wonder how Bunyan could so articulately and creatively express the emotions of anxiety and despair that frequently checker the Christian life—but all my questions came to rest when I learned that the story's characters (such as Giant Despair) and locations (such as Doubting Castle) were not created in a vacuum but were rooted in the author's personal experience.

A Life of Grief

John Bunyan's bestseller was written not from a corner office but from the prison cell that was his home for twelve years. He was imprisoned for preaching the gospel. He was free to go at any point—so long as he promised to never preach the gospel again. Bunyan's love for Christ and his passion for the gospel propelled him to respond, "I have determined . . . yet to suffer, if frail life might continue so long, even till the moss shall grow on my eyebrows, rather than thus to violate my faith and principles."[1] What an example of boldness and faithfulness! Especially considering the trials Bunyan was enduring: two years prior to his incarceration at Bedford prison, Bunyan's first wife died—leaving behind four young children—one of whom was blind. A year later, Bunyan remarried, and even though he grieved the loss of his first wife, he rejoiced in God's provision of a second. Following his imprisonment, however, Bunyan's pregnant and distressed new bride, Elizabeth, went into early labor and, after eight days, gave birth to a stillborn child.

Bunyan heard the news in his prison cell. His wife was grieving the loss of her baby, his children were still grieving the loss of their mother, and Bunyan's own heart was broken.

Can you imagine? Going through such heartache and pain all while being separated from your loved ones?

Maybe you can. Maybe you've been there. Not in the Bedford prison, but in the dungeon of despair that comes from gut-wrenching pain and harrowing loss. Bunyan wrote honestly about the despondency and desolation he faced during this difficult time: "The parting with my wife and poor children hath oft been to me in this place as the pulling the flesh from my bones." He went on to say that the combination of his wife's sorrow, his child's death, and his blind daughter's suffering was enough to "break my heart to pieces."[2]

While sitting in his dark, damp, and dreary cell, Bunyan missed his children's childhood, his wife, and his church family. Year after year for more than a decade, Bunyan, like anyone else, would have asked, *Where is God at times like these? Is He really in control?*

Where Is God?

Your suffering may not be on par with John Bunyan's, but you may ask the same questions: "Where is God, and *who* is in control?" Kingdoms are tottering. Enemy nations claim to be test-firing nuclear weapons systems.[3] Food and fuel prices are soaring. My company is downsizing. Civilization is failing. And, on top of that, my washing machine is broken! *Where is God and who is in control?* Maybe as you survey the landscape of our chaotic world and your chaotic life, your mind fills with worry and anxiety—and maybe, at the peak of your worry and fear, someone tells you: "Just trust God."

Initially, you may respond with an affirmative nod, but over time you wonder, *Is this whole idea of trusting God simply Christian mumbo jumbo? Is God trustworthy? Is He actually in control?*

John Bunyan asked these same questions in his prison cell. Bunyan admitted that he was often afflicted with anxiety and also knew that as a child of God he was commanded to "trust in the LORD" (Proverbs 3:5)—but like anyone who endures difficulty, pain, and trouble, Bunyan asked his own heart, *How? How can I trust God? Is He really in control?* Maybe as you reflect on the heartache and uncertainty of your life, you identify with Bunyan's yearning question: *Where is God in dark times?*

In his book *Seasonable Counsel, or Advice to Sufferers,* Bunyan shared the truth that was most precious, comforting, and invigorating to him during this difficult time: the sovereignty of God.

Amid the waves of adversity and the gut-wrenching pain of loss, God's sovereignty was the solid rock that Bunyan clung to. When confined to the darkness of his prison cell and when wrestling with the black anxiety and despair of his heart, Bunyan had only one hope: *my God is sovereign.*

Now, you've likely heard the term *sovereign,* but what does it even mean—especially as it relates to God? Before I provide a definition of God's sovereignty, can I encourage you? You need to grasp and then meditate on this lofty truth of your heavenly Father—especially if you are walking through the valley. The sovereignty of God is indeed a hard doctrine to grapple with, but it provides the softest comfort and surest hope to the anxious and despairing.

So back to our question: What does it mean that God is sovereign?

Simply put, God's sovereignty means that He is the supreme authority in the universe. It means that He is in control. It means that He ordains, orders, and orchestrates all things for His glory and His children's eternal good. Our world abounds with chaos, but in heaven there is no panic, only our Father's perfect plans. The Bible teaches that even the situations, circumstances, and people who have prompted our pain are under the sovereign control and purposeful orchestration of our heavenly Father.

Do you believe this?

We are going to unpack the scope, extent, and meaning of God's sovereignty as this chapter unfolds, but for a moment I want to draw your attention to the reality that if God is *not* sovereign, if He is not in control, then we have all the reason in the world to be anxious. If there is no divine plan for our adversity and affliction, then we have no hope in the midst of it—only madness and pain. Our confusion is compounded, our anxiety is accelerated, and our fear is fueled when we strip the anchoring doctrine of God's sovereignty from our lives and fail to set our minds on its truth. To clarify, God's sovereignty does not eliminate anguish and grief from our lives, but it does allow us to adopt the Christian's motto of "sorrowful yet always rejoicing" (2 Corinthians 6:10). In my own life, I don't know how I could live a single day (especially a difficult one) without hiding myself in the shelter of my Father's rule and reign.

Sovereign over All

Just how sovereign is God? Sovereign in all things? Or only the good things? What about the hard things? What about my pain?

My wife and I recently found out that she was pregnant with our third baby! We beamed with excitement and wondered: Would it be a boy? Or maybe a third baby girl? But three days ago Caity called me crying. I could tell something was wrong before she even had to say it: "Jonny, I think I just miscarried." My heart sank. Is God sovereign over that? What about over catastrophes? Cancer? Suffering? The future? I want to answer these questions throughout the rest of the chapter. Prayerfully, I hope to do so with the tenderness and compassion of Jesus without compromising the clarity and authority with which He speaks in His Word.

The Bible answers our question "How sovereign is God?"

Psalm 103:19 says, "The LORD has established His throne in the heavens, and His sovereignty rules over all." In Hebrew, the verb translated "rules" is in the present perfect tense, which means that God's rule and sovereignty never had a beginning and, consequently, will never have an end.

Empires fall.

Dynasties die.

Presidents can be impeached.

Kings can be overthrown.

But God is on the throne, and He is not going anywhere. He does not slumber (Psalm 121:4–5). He takes no sabbaticals. He *rules*. Maybe you have walked through dark times and deep shadows, maybe you are walking through great tragedy even now, but Scripture reminds us that there has never been a single moment in your life wherein God was not actively *ruling*—not only over the universe, but over your life. God is not a figurehead who merely possesses the title of "king" and poses for pictures. He possesses absolute authority, and He exercises that authority at every moment of every day for all eternity. And do you know what? God is proud of this. Throughout the Bible, God is never shy, sheepish, or self-deprecating as it relates to declaring His sovereign power. Consider

Isaiah 46:9, where God said, "I am God, and there is no other; I am God, and there is *no one like Me*" (emphasis added).

Now, if you were to ask, *What makes God so different from everyone and everything else? Since He says, "There is no one like Me," what makes Him so separate, so holy, and so unlike His creatures?*

God Himself answers that question in the next verse in Isaiah 46, where He says that he "declar[es] the end from the beginning, and from ancient times things which have not been done, saying, 'My purpose will be established, and I will accomplish all My good pleasure'" (v. 10).

So, what exactly makes God unlike all others?

His sovereignty.

He declares the end from the beginning and none of His plans are thwarted or frustrated by anything in the natural or supernatural world. Have you ever wondered what makes God, God? If so, the answer would be that He and He alone is the ultimate sovereign of the universe. Scripture gives you a big truth anchor to stabilize your soul: your Father rules. This means that everything in the remotest galaxy and everything in *your* life is held firmly in His powerful hand.

Now, again, if you don't believe that God is in control, what's at stake? Well, for one, if He is not sovereign, then you cannot trust Him. If God is not *in* control, then our entire lives are *out of control*, and we are left straining and striving to control all things ourselves—which only serves to perpetuate our anxiety and fear. Moreover, a failure to fix our gaze on the sovereignty of our heavenly Father not only accelerates our anxiety, but it diminishes the entirety of the way we view God's character. Why? Because our Father's sovereignty is necessary for any of His other attributes to have value or meaning to us. For example, if God is good and kind but lacks the sovereignty to extend and express His goodness and kindness, what good would His goodness be? If He is wise but lacks the sovereignty to carry out the wisdom of His will, what good would His wisdom be? If He is love, but His hands are tied and His fingers crossed because He lacks control, the value of His love would be diminished, and the entirety of His character would be distorted. Can I put it to you this way? If God is not sovereign, He is not God.

Remember how we defined the exercise of faith as *gazing at God*? One of the truths God wants to ground our thinking in and set our gaze on is our Father's sovereign rule and reign. Anxiety asks, "What if?" God's Word says, "Your Father is in control." Jesus repeatedly affirmed these precious and powerful truths to His fearful and anxious followers. As Jesus comforted His anxious followers, He told them to look at the birds of the air, and then later, in Matthew 10:29–30, He made a stunning statement: "Are not two sparrows sold for a penny? And not one of them will fall to the ground apart from your Father. But even the hairs of your head are all numbered" (ESV). Immediately prior to this statement, Jesus twice told his disciples not to fear (Matthew 10:26, 28), and then He gave them the reason why: *our* Father is sovereign. Sparrows weigh less than an ounce—they are worth less than half a cent (Luke 12:6)—and do you know what? Not one of them lives or dies outside of God's complete control. Jesus routinely employed lesser-to-greater reasoning throughout the Gospels—remember, He wanted the disciples to *think*. He wants His followers to reason within their own minds and ask: *If God is sovereign over seemingly insignificant sparrows, how much more is He sovereign over those whom He has made in His own image? If two sparrows are sold for a cent, how much more will God guide and govern those whom He has bought with the precious blood of His one and only Son?*

Before continuing in our examination of our Father's rule and reign, can you observe one other element about the words of Jesus we have just examined? Jesus detailed that our Father is sovereign over the stars, the sparrows, and everything in between, and then

He added, "Do not fear; you are more valuable than many sparrows" (Luke 12:7). Take note of this: the Bible never segregates God's sovereignty from His love and care for His children. In Isaiah 40 we read that God is the one who "measured the waters in the hollow of His hand," who "marked off the heavens by the span," and to whom "the nations are like a drop from a bucket" and "the islands like fine dust" (vv. 12, 15). The passage goes on to say that God "sits above the circle of the earth, and its inhabitants are like grasshoppers" to the One who "stretches out the heavens like a curtain" (v. 22) and calls the stars "by name" (v. 26).

But do you want to know what's amazing about these verses?

It's not just that they display God's power, majesty, and sovereignty, it's that these features of God's rule are tethered to these preceding words: "Like a shepherd He will tend His flock, in His arm He will gather the lambs and carry them in His bosom; He will gently lead the nursing ewes" (Isaiah 40:11). God is a powerful ruler, and He is a gentle Shepherd. Keep both realities in mind as you continue to read. It's only by holding all of these truths simultaneously that we can heed the imperative exhortation by our Lord: "Do not fear."

The Scope of God's Sovereignty

Let me ask you again, just how sovereign is God? Psalm 103:19 says that God's sovereignty rules over "all." In examining what exactly is included under "all," I want to survey Scripture and detail several areas over which God exercises His sovereign authority. If God is not sovereign over *one* of these areas, He cannot be sovereign in the others. If He were sovereign over man but not sovereign over Satan, how could He be in control over man if Satan had the power to thwart and frustrate His purposes? As we will observe, however, there is not a single molecule, nor a single man, nor a single super-natural being in all of creation that is outside the sovereign rule of our heavenly Father. If you are anxious, pray that God will grant you a magnified conviction of His control even as you read this. If you are in great trial or deep affliction, or facing what may seem to be unbearable sorrow, pray this way: *Lord, help me to believe You are sovereign and loving and have the power to redeem all my pain and brokenness and that You have a perfect plan for Your glory and my good.*

God Is Sovereign over Kings and Kingdoms

Are you anxious about our country's future? Are you fearful about the plans of enemy nations? Do you think our civilization is on the brink of destruction? Then find comfort and peace in this: God rules and reigns over every nation, every king, and every kingdom.

The most powerful kingdom on earth is like a dandelion that God eviscerates and eliminates with His own breath (Isaiah 40:24). He "removes kings and establishes kings" (Daniel 2:21), and the heart of every king is like "channels of water in the hand of the LORD; He turns it wherever He wishes" (Proverbs 21:1). In ancient times a king operated outside any other authority—there was no supreme court to restrain him or any chamber or counsel that would keep his authority in check. And yet even the most stouthearted men such as kings are as malleable as playdough in the hands of God. Again, "The king's heart is like channels of water in the hand of the LORD; He turns it wherever He wishes."

Consider the following examples in the Bible:

1. God moved the heart of the pagan king Cyrus so that the people of God could rebuild the temple wall (Ezra 1:1–3).
2. God gave King Xerxes sleeplessness so that he called for the chronicle of his reign to be read and was reminded to reward

Esther's uncle Mordecai, the very man Haman had planned to assassinate.

3. God hardened Pharaoh's heart so that His glory and power would be put on display through the plagues.
4. God moved the hearts of Babylonian officials to show Daniel favor and sympathy (Daniel 1:9).

Scripture is clear—God is sovereign over kings and kingdoms. Why? Because He is sovereign over *every single individual*. No emperor, boss, manager, or CEO has any power unless it has been given to him or her by our sovereign and loving God. Even those who are bent on hurting us or harming us cannot touch us unless God first grants permission. God is in control, not just in the favorable dispositions, but also in the unfavorable. Jesus told Pilate, "You would have no authority over Me, unless it had been given you from above" (John 19:11). This provides the believer with great confidence and security even when facing persecution or the unknown. Satan seeks to destroy the children of God in the jaws of suffering, but even the believer's subjection to persecution is according to the will of God (1 Peter 4:19).

Perhaps you're wondering, *Does this mean man is not responsible?* No, it does not—man *is* responsible. The Bible asserts both God's sovereignty and mankind's moral responsibility. Presidents, prime ministers, and crowned kings do not contradict God's plan but fulfill it, and in doing so they are not being coerced by God but acting according to their own volition. For example, there are numerous instances in the book of Exodus where God said He was going to harden Pharaoh's heart (Exodus 4:21; 7:3; 9:12; 10:1, 20, 27; 11:10; 14:4, 8); however, there are also multiple instances where it says that Pharaoh *hardened his own heart* (7:13, 22; 8:15, 19, 32; 9:7, 34–35). God is sovereign, but man is responsible. As followers of Christ, we are not attempting to *reconcile* God's sovereignty with man's responsibility (because they are not at odds); we are *recognizing* that they are twin truths that stand side by side.

God's sovereignty over all individuals means that He never has to operate like a skilled coach who calls divine audibles when things don't go as planned. God has never been caught off guard, nor has He been surprised by kings and kingdoms. He rules over them. Jerry Bridges stated: "Confidence in this area of God's sovereignty is crucial for if there is a single event or single person or single nation that is operating outside of God's sovereignty, you cannot trust him."[4] God may love you, He may be good, but you cannot entrust yourself to Him unless He rules and reigns over all kings, kingdoms, and individuals.

God Is Sovereign over Nature

Not only is God sovereign over nations, but He also rules and reigns over everything in nature. No baby is born (Psalm 139:13), no sparrow dies (Matthew 10:29), no lightning strikes (Job 38:35), no stars shift their positions (38:31–32), no wave crashes (38:11), no drop of rain falls (38:26), no lion hunts (38:39), and no hawk soars (39:26) apart from God's sovereign rule. God not only can hush the proudest of kings (Daniel 4), but He can also hush the wind and the seas and they immediately obey Him (Mark 4). In the book of Jonah, God "hurled" a great wind (Jonah 1:4 ESV), then "appointed" a great fish to swallow Jonah (1:17 ESV); then God told that fish to vomit Jonah onto dry land (2:10); then God prepared a tall plant to give Jonah shade (4:6), then a worm to eat that plant (4:7), and then a "scorching east wind" to blow (4:8). Much more could be said, but it must be understood that, contrary to what David Attenborough tells you as he narrates *Planet Earth*, we are not victim to random acts of "mother nature"; we are under the sovereign orchestration of God. If no sparrow falls to the ground outside His permission, then can we not be sure that no tornado whirls and no earthquake strikes outside of God's sovereign decree? God is the one who "causes His sun to rise on the evil and the good, and sends rain on the righteous and the unrighteous" (Matthew 5:45). Although there are physical laws operating in nature, those physical laws exist only to do the will of the Lawgiver, who is sovereign over every sparrow and every storm.

Is it raining outside? God sent the rain (Matthew 5:45).

Is the sun shining? God causes the sun to shine (Matthew 5:45).

Our sovereign God created the world, sustains the world, and will one day soon remake the world (Revelation 21:5).

God Is Sovereign over Time

As Bunyan sat in his prison cell for more than a decade, these words must have brought him comfort amid his pain: "All the days ordained for me were written in your book before one of them came to be" (Psalm 139:16 NIV). God not only knows when we will be born and when we will die, but He also knows and controls every day in between that is riddled with despair and fraught with worry.

At this juncture we must consider: *If there was a single moment in your life when God was not sovereign, could you trust Him? Could you give your undying allegiance to a God that was inconsistent in His control?*

No. No you could not.

But God can be trusted because He reigns supreme over every ticking of the clock. We don't even know what our lives will look like tomorrow (James 4:13), and we may be prone to worry about what tomorrow will bring, but the God who holds the future tells us, "Do not worry about tomorrow" (Matthew 6:34 NIV). Why? Because our Father holds tomorrow, the day after tomorrow, and all of time, for that matter, in His sovereign hand.

God Is Sovereign over Suffering

Margaret Clarkson was born in 1915 and endured much pain and hardship throughout her life. She initially suffered from constant migraines that later turned into convulsions and vomiting. In her book *Destined for Glory*, she wrote that her mother informed her that her first words were "My head hurts."[5] By age three, Margaret was bedbound because of her crippling arthritis, and in her book she reflected on the bald spot she had on the back of her head—not as a result of a biotin deficiency but as a consequence of lying in bed for such great lengths of time. Although her pain was intermittent throughout her youth, her loneliness was not. She longed and prayed for a husband, but Margaret was single her entire life. Whether it was financial hardship, physical pain, or relational loneliness, Margaret's life was seemingly tethered to suffering until her death in 2008. What gave her the strength to go on? What gave her hope amid her loneliness and pain?

In her book *Grace Grows Best in Winter*, Margaret Clarkson wrote these words:

> The sovereignty of God is the one impregnable rock to which the suffering human heart must cling. The circumstances surrounding our lives are no accident; they may be the work of evil, but that evil is held firmly within the mighty hand of our sovereign God. . . . All evil is subject to Him, and evil cannot touch His children unless He permits it. God is the Lord of human history and of the personal history of every member of His redeemed family.[6]

Clarkson continued to explain that the believer must encounter every ounce of adversity in this life with this perspective: "We set ourselves to believe in the overruling goodness, providence, and sovereignty of God and refuse to turn aside no matter what may come, no matter how we feel."[7]

The only comfort in our suffering is that the God who loves us is sovereign over it all. I'm so thankful that no hardship in my life has ever occurred outside my heavenly Father's control. Even those who intend to harm us, God can use it for His glory and our good (Genesis 50:20). God is not attempting to salvage our suffering so that it has some remnant of redeeming value; He is the orchestrator behind it all. Satan may intend to sift us like wheat (Luke 22:31), but God preserves and protects those who are His. Satan may use the rocky places of affliction and persecution in an attempt to strip those in the church from God and His Word (Matthew 13:21), but God will uphold those who belong to Him. Why? Because our suffering is in the hands of a sovereign God.

Why does disaster come to a certain city? "Is a trumpet blown in a city, and the people are not afraid? Does disaster come to a city, unless the LORD has done it?" (Amos 3:6 ESV).

Why are some babies born healthy and some with spina bifida? "The LORD said to him, 'Who has made man's mouth? Or who makes him mute or deaf, or seeing or blind? Is it not I, the LORD?'" (Exodus 4:11).

Suffering is not the checkmate to God's sovereignty but rather a piece in the grandmaster's hands. The pawn can have hope and live by faith, knowing that, in the end, there is a plan behind the problems we face. Maybe this is discomforting to you to hear that God is sovereign even over suffering, but let me tell you this: there is no comfort in suffering unless God is sovereign over it. We must learn to trust that God is working out His plan, even when we can't connect the dots. *Are you in pain? Have you experienced great affliction? Do you grieve the loss of those you once held dear?* Scripture says there is no trial, no tear shed, no diagnosis, and no unjust firing outside of a sovereign God who is also infinite in His wisdom and perfect in His love.

God Is Sovereign over Satan and Evil

In the first chapter of Job, Sabeans, Chaldeans, wind, and fire destroy Job's family, livestock, and servants. There is an element of dramatic irony at play in the opening chapter of Job where the readers know more about what is happening than Job does. If we read through the events without the context given to us by the writer, we may be tempted to ask: Where was God amid such tragedy? In reading the opening verses of the book, however, we find God to be in the same place He always is—on the throne.

God was not caught off guard by these attacks or by Job's pain. Before Satan attacked Job, God first granted permission. God was the one who asked Satan, "Have you considered My servant Job?" (1:8). Satan responded, "Does Job fear God for nothing? Have You not made a hedge about him and his house and all that he has, on every side?" (vv. 9–10). *You have blessed him, protected him, given him wealth—no wonder he loves You. Let me take it all away, and then Job will curse Your name.*

What happened next?

God granted permission (v. 12).

Job's life was destroyed, and in the final verse of the first chapter, we read: "Through all this Job did not sin nor did he blame God" (v. 22).

Then what happened?

Satan returned to God, acknowledged Job's perseverance and righteousness, then made a new proposition to God: "Skin for skin! Yes, all that a man has he will give for his life. However, put forth Your hand now, and touch his bone and his flesh; he will curse You to Your face" (Job 2:4–5).

Then what?

God granted permission, saying, "Behold, he is in your power, only spare his life" (v. 6).

We find Job in the aftermath—heartbroken, sitting in a pile of dirt, scraping his boils with a potsherd, as his wife tells him to "curse God and die" (v. 9).

Stay with me here.

You need to understand—Satan and God are not wrestling back and forth in a cosmic tug-of-war. There is indeed a spiritual war being waged, but the battle between God and Satan is not Rocky versus Drago, where one throws a punch and the other punches back. God is completely sovereign over the devil. Satan is a runt pawn, and God is *the* king. Furthermore, in the account of Job, God didn't answer questions, He *asked* them. God didn't ask for permission, He *granted* it. God didn't present Himself before Satan, Satan presented himself before the King. It's crucial to understand that, in a world of darkness, Yahweh is not straining His divine muscles against a formidable foe. He is completely sovereign over Satan. The devil does indeed have measurable influence in this world—he is referred to as "the ruler of this world" (John 12:31), "the god of this world" (2 Corinthians 4:4), and the "prince of the power of the air" (Ephesians 2:2), but the authority Satan exercises is subject to God's permission and to the limits that God has set.[8] Sometimes people find greater comfort in thinking Satan is more sovereign than God because that gives them someone to blame, but may I ask you—do you really want to go there? Do you really want to believe that Satan exercises authority over God or that Satan does *anything* apart from God's permission?[9] John Piper said, "Satan cannot move without God loosening his leash."[10] Evil has not gotten "out of hand" for God, and no evil that has come your way has frustrated the plans of God. Again, this is not to say that God is the author of evil, nor does He condone evil, but He allows, uses, and ordains evil to accomplish His good purpose.

Sometimes on a quest to get God off the hook for evil, we may be tempted to deny what is explicit in the Bible and assert the idea that God's hands are "clean," as it were, in relation to the evil in our world. Perhaps you, like Job, may wonder, *How can a good and powerful God allow such evil in my life and in the lives of others?* Some have claimed that God can be either good and kind, or sovereign, but not both—stating that if He was sovereign *and* good, then evil wouldn't exist. For many years this reality of evil and the sovereignty of God has been called the Achilles' heel of the Christian faith. When we look to the Bible, however, we see that the "problem of evil" is no problem for God. God *does* hate and grieve over the evil that abounds in our world, but God does not need a publicist to protect Him from the accusations people bring against His sovereign rule— nor does Scripture ever elevate man's freedom to the degree that our heavenly Father is featured as a hands-tied and feet-bound deity trying His best to control evil but keeps falling short.

Consider for a moment the following passages:

> Lamentations 3:37–38, God says, "Who is there who speaks
> and it comes to pass, unless the Lord has commanded it?
> Is it not from the mouth of the Most High that both good
> and ill go forth?"
> Isaiah 45:6–7, "I am the LORD, and there is no other, the One
> forming light and creating darkness, causing well-being
> and creating calamity; I am the LORD who does all these."
> Ephesians 1:11, "Having been predestined according to
> His purpose who works all things after the counsel of
> His will."

To deny God's absolute sovereignty over evil is to deny the Bible and diminish our Father's character. God's sovereignty is not limited a single degree by human freedom or by supernatural powers—nor is He caught off guard by evil. Man *is* responsible, yet man's responsibility never nullifies God's sovereignty. The Westminster Confession of Faith (1646) addresses the twin truths of man's responsibility and God's sovereignty by saying, "God, from all eternity, did, by the most wise and holy counsel of His own will, freely, and unchangeably ordain whatsoever comes to pass: yet so, as thereby neither is God the author of sin, nor is violence offered to the will of the creatures; nor is the liberty or contingency of second causes taken away, but rather established" (3.1). What does this mean? That God is sovereign over evil, yet He can never be blamed for evil for He Himself is good. Furthermore, man will be held responsible before God for all the evil they perform.

Following his suffering, Job called God to the court of his own justice and began to ask questions of God. Interestingly, God responded to Job's questioning, not by *answering* Job's questions, but by *asking* him questions that would cause him to consider the character of God:

Did you create the world (Job 38:4)?
Do you command the morning (Job 38:12)?
Do you bind the stars (Job 38:31)?
Do you command the lightning (Job 38:35)?
Do you hunt the prey for the lion (Job 38:39)?
Do you control the dinosaurs (Job 40:15–24)?

God continued for four chapters, and Job finally responded in Job 42:2, saying, "I know that You can do all things, and that no purpose of Yours can be thwarted."

Job did not blame Satan for the evil that he endured. Yes, the Chaldeans and Sabeans were complicit in his suffering, but Job knew behind it all was the hand of God. Many have claimed that the only way to endure such tragic levels of pain is to deny God's involvement altogether, but it's only in coming to terms with God's rule and reign, even over evil, that we will be able to say with Job, "Though He slay me, I will hope in Him" (Job 13:15). Only when we understand that no purpose of God's can be thwarted will we have confidence that His goodness will be able to bring light to harsh and dark times.

The truth of God's sovereignty over evil is a difficult doctrine to grapple with, and you may be wondering at this juncture, *If God is sovereign, why does He allow evil?* Although worthy of a much longer response, in Scripture we see that God allows evil for three main reasons: to reveal His righteousness (Romans 3:5), to reveal His glory (Ephesians 1:6), and to reveal His love (Romans 5:8). Because of the weight and depth of this subject, I sat down with fellow pastor and author Scott Christensen (who has written three books on God's sovereignty) and asked him this very question: *Why does our sovereign God allow evil?*

Here is what he said: "We don't always know why God allows evil. But we do know that God Himself is always good. Furthermore, we know this: God never allows any evil to take place that does not facilitate a greater good that could not have happened unless that evil had taken place."[11]

For example, what's the most egregious evil ever committed in human history? The slaughter of Jesus Christ. Consequently, what's the greatest good ever extended to mankind? The redemption of lost sinners. Do you see? There at the cross the most horrific evil facilitated the greatest good, which resulted in the greatest glory for God. In 2 Timothy 1:9 we read one of the striking revelations of Scripture—that God purposed to extend His grace to us "in Christ Jesus from all eternity." Which means this: if God's grace was given to us before the beginning of time (and, therefore, before the fall of man), then we must know that God knew evil would exist and had a plan to shine the riches of His grace, glory, and love against the backdrop of human evil.

Are you anxious that the devil is out to get you or those you love? Are you worried that you will be the target of evil in this world? Satan and evil cannot touch you without first asking your heavenly Father for permission. True statements, however, are not always easy to swallow. Nor should we go guns blazing with these truths to people who have been on the receiving end of tragic evil. As I write this chapter, multiple people in my own church have experienced horrific evil and heartbreaking loss, and at times it may seem easier, or more comforting, to look at Satan as the sovereign rather than God because that gives us someone to blame. But the Bible blasts the notion of a hands-tied, impotent God by stating plainly that Satan's power never supersedes that of God's. Pol Pot, Hitler, and Stalin were agents of satanic evil in this world, but they were not operating outside of God's sovereign control. At times we may tend to humanize God as if He were just as surprised and flummoxed as we are by the evil in our world, but the Bible never presents God in this manner. Our world does groan under the reality and presence of evil. Our hearts break over the injustice and pain that we may have endured. Thankfully, the One who drove the demons into the pigs (Matthew 8:31) will one day cast Satan forevermore into the lake of fire (Revelation 20:10) and crush Satan under our feet (Romans 16:20).

Pieces of Pie

At times the knowledge of God's sovereignty can compound our suffering rather than calm our hearts when His rule and reign are not appropriately conjoined with His other attributes. For example, during my time in Australia, my friend Micah received a call from his dad: "It's Mom. Her breast cancer is back."

Micah flew home immediately. I followed two days later. Within twenty-four hours of my arrival back in California, "Momma Dixon," as we called her, had gone to be with the Lord. The cancer that was in remission had returned and taken the life of the mom, piano teacher, choir director, and gracious host that so many people had loved. I remember watching someone come up to Micah at his mother's memorial service, pat him on the shoulder, and say, "God is sovereign." This much is true. But bare and glib expressions do not

Consider the Lilies

help us unless we know that the One who is sovereign over our suffering also holds our tears in a bottle (Psalm 56:8), knows our names (Isaiah 43:1), loves us immensely (Romans 5:8), and has a plan that is for His glory and our eternal good (Romans 8:28).[12]

For this reason it is so important that we don't look at God's attributes like various pieces of a pie. Again, God is not 50 percent love, 25 percent sovereign, 10 percent just, and so forth. He is all of His attributes, all the time, in full measure. Therefore, in examining God's sovereignty, we cannot divorce this attribute of God from His wisdom—or His goodness. If the plan that God is working all things toward is not one that is also infinitely wise, and infinitely good, then we can never walk by faith and not by sight. But as Paul said in Romans 11:33, "Oh, the depth of the riches both of the wisdom and knowledge of God!" Moreover, in tethering God's sovereignty to His love, we find comfort and peace in the fact that God will never exercise His sovereignty outside of His personal care for us. He does not make flippant decisions that are indifferent to our welfare. "He does not afflict willingly or grieve the sons of men" (Lamentations 3:33). This means that God finds no joy in bringing pain and grief into the lives of those He loves—as a Father, He grieves to see us grieve.

Have you ever considered the fact that Jesus cried at Lazarus's grave immediately prior to resurrecting him from the dead? Isn't this interesting? Why would Jesus cry when He knew that He was about to bring Lazarus back to life? Why didn't Jesus say, "Hey, everybody, check this out! Watch this!" Rather, the passage says that "Jesus wept" (John 11:35). Profusely. And the question is "Why?" Do you know the answer? Because He is not a distant God. He is a sympathetic high priest (Hebrews 4:15). He feels what we feel. He knows what we are going through. He loves and cares for us. He Himself was a "man of sorrows and acquainted with grief" (Isaiah 53:3 ESV). He is sovereign, but His sovereignty is always anchored to His love and care.

Working Out All Things for Good

Sometimes well-intentioned people go up to those who are suffering and tell them, "God is going to work it all out for good." After all, Scripture says as much in Romans 8:28: "We know that God causes all things to work together for good to those who love God, to those who are called according to His purpose." But what is the "good" that God is working all things toward? Well, in Scripture, the answer we are looking for is routinely found in the next verse. Romans 8:29 tells us the "good" that God is working all things toward and the grand plan He has for our lives—do you know what it is?

"For those whom He foreknew, He also predestined to become conformed to the image of His Son, so that He would be the first-born among many brethren."

Did you catch that?

What is God's plan for our good and His glory?

Our conformation into the image of His Son, Jesus Christ.

How can we say, "Happy is the man whom God reproves" (Job 5:17), unless we trust that God is using the dark threads and deep knots in our lives to transform us into the image of the Savior whom we love? Scripture teaches us that our suffering is not for nothing. Our deepest lessons are learned from the deepest suffering.[13] Gold must first pass through the fire to be pure, and believers are similarly refined in the furnace of affliction. C. S. Lewis, in his book *The Problem of Pain*, wrote, "God whispers to us in our pleasures, speaks in our conscience, but shouts in our pain: it is His megaphone to rouse a deaf world."[14] In your own life, what are the times and seasons you have most grown in your trust and relationship with God? I venture to say that it is not in times of great blessing but rather in times of profound difficulty and pain. In our suffering, God rarely answers the *why* of our suffering, but He answers *who* is behind it all. And because He is sovereign over our suffering, He alone is able to sustain and uphold us when we walk through the valley. At times, as in the case with Paul, God's glory, sufficiency, and strength shine most brightly on the stage of human inadequacy—His power is made perfect in our weakness (2 Corinthians 12:9).

We still doubt, and our faith falters. We ask, *How can I really know that my sovereign God is good and kind?*

Because in the sovereignty of God, He sent forth His Son to die for your sin. The Bible says that at the proper time (Galatians 4:4) Jesus was born of a virgin, lived a perfect and sinless life (1 Peter 2:22), and then died at the hands of those He came to save. He was in one sense *murdered*, but it must be understood that Jesus *came to die*. He went willingly to the cross (Isaiah 53:7). He was not forced. Yes, Jesus was killed by human hands, but He was "delivered over by the predetermined plan and foreknowledge of God" (Acts 2:23). The crucifixion wasn't a wrinkle in God's plan, it *was* God's plan. The cross of Calvary preaches the strongest sermon ever on the sovereignty of God. There, the most unjust suffering was endured by the most innocent person. There, the suffering Son of God was forsaken by His Father (Matthew 27:46), so that when you come to Him in your suffering, you do so, not as one who is forsaken by God, but as one who is held in His saving, sovereign, and loving hand.

My Life Is but a Weaving

Perhaps you are familiar with the life and testimony of Corrie ten Boom—her family was arrested in their attempt to help the Jews escape from the Nazis during the Holocaust. While imprisoned at the Ravensbrück concentration camp, Corrie's sister Betsie died, and by the time the war was over, three other members of her family had also died in German prisons. Sitting in the dark cell of an oppressive and brutal prison camp, Corrie was tempted to worry, she was prone to despair, but it was the truth of God's sovereignty that enabled her to trust God—to walk by faith, even when she could not see.

Songwriter and poet George Colfax Tullar's best-known poem is titled "The Weaver." In the poem, Tullar compares our lives to the underside of a tapestry where everything appears to be in disarray and in want of order, but we see only the "under side"; the weaver sees the "upper." Our Father is the Weaver, He is good, and He knows what He is doing. The children of God can entrust their lives to the Weaver, who uses "dark threads" so that He can weave a tapestry that is for His glory and for our good. Our Father is sovereign, and yet He also knows us, loves us, and cares for us (1 Peter 5:7). Are you anxious? Are you despairing? Then "trust in the LORD with all your heart and do not lean on your own understanding. In all your ways acknowledge Him, and He will make your paths straight" (Proverbs 3:5–6). Our Father is sovereign over kings and kingdoms, sparrows, and storms, suffering and pain, Satan and all evil, and in His sovereignty, He sent His one and only Son, Jesus Christ, to die for your sin—you can trust Him.

> My Life is but a weaving
> Between my Lord and me;
> I cannot choose the colors
> He worketh steadily.
> Oft times He weaveth sorrow
> And I, in foolish pride,
> Forget He sees the upper,
> And I the under side.
> Not til the loom is silent
> And the shuttles cease to fly,
> Shall God unroll the canvas
> And explain the reason why.
> The dark threads are as needful

> In the Weaver's skillful hand,
> As the threads of gold and silver
> In the pattern He has planned.
> He knows, He loves, He cares,
> Nothing this truth can dim.
> He gives His very best to those
> Who chose to walk with Him.[15]

— Reflection Questions —

1. If God is really the ruler of all things, how should that affect our feelings or anxiety about politics, finances, relationships, or other common sources of worry? (Read Proverbs 21:1.)

2. Many of you have walked through deep seasons of suffering—if God was not sovereign over your suffering, what hope would you have in the midst (or aftermath) of the pain that you endured? Why do you think Margaret Clarkson wrote, "The sovereignty of God is the one impregnable rock to which the suffering human heart must cling." Why does God's sovereignty *over* and *in* our suffering anchor us with hope amid the storms of this life?

3. How do people commonly misinterpret and misapply Romans 8:28? What is the "good" God is working all things out for (v. 29)? Why does an accurate understanding of God's eternal plan (v. 30) help us to trust Him in the here and now?

CHAPTER 10

Lavish Love

The Christmas holiday is cherished because it's a time to reflect on our Savior's birth, behold His love, and experience His goodness as we gather with the people we cherish. The season is filled with celebration and festivities, and the Christmas spirit is cued by the lights and evergreens in the spaces and places around us. Of course, people also anticipate the season because it is a time to give and receive gifts from their friends and loved ones. (I'll never forget receiving my Michael Jordan jersey when I was a kid.)

According to PR Newswire, 34 percent of Americans purchase gifts for their dogs.

Twenty-two percent of Americans purchase gifts for their cats.

Meanwhile . . . only 19 percent of Americans purchase gifts for their in-laws.[1] Yes, people are more likely to spend money on "Tom and Jerry" than they are on "Bob and Mary."

Each Christmas, people often poke fun at the dynamics at play in their relationships with their in-laws (thankfully, mine are great), but it would be hard to think of anyone in the Bible who had a tenser and more difficult relationship with their father-in-law than Israel's King David.

After marrying King Saul's daughter, David's popularity began to soar. Saul's heart became jealous and insecure, and David's relationship with Saul quickly deteriorated. David was anointed the next king of Israel as a teenager, but do you how he spent the following decade?

Running for his life, hiding in caves, and foraging for food as his father-in-law Saul sought to kill him.

At one point, with Saul's army on his tail, David became so desperate in his flight from Saul that he sought refuge among the Philistines—the home of Goliath, the warrior he had killed. This is how low David had been brought in life. He felt safer behind enemy lines than he did with his family. David had experienced moments of anxiety and fear before, but perhaps none exceeded this episode in which he was caught between a rock and a hard place. Saul was scouring the wilderness looking to kill David, and the citizens of Gath, who, after seeing David come into their city, said to one another, "Isn't he the one they sing about in their dances: 'Saul has slain his thousands, and David his tens of thousands'?" (1 Samuel 21:10–15 NIV). *Isn't this the guy who killed our greatest warrior? If you were David, how would you feel in such a scenario?*

In Psalm 34, David recounted how God protected him during this difficult time. David's soul was badgered and yet he burst forth in praise, saying, "Oh, taste and see that the LORD is good! Blessed is the man who takes refuge in him!" (v. 8 ESV). Interestingly, David detailed that the surest weapon at his disposal during this difficult time was not the sword of Goliath (1 Samuel 21:9), nor was it his mighty men around him (2 Samuel 23:8–39), but it was something else entirely. Goliath's sword may have been able to cut through armor, but it couldn't dent the rising fear within David's mind. His soldiers may have protected him from outside enemies, but they could not protect David from the assailant of anxiety within. For that type or protection and strength, David needed something stronger than steel and mightier than iron: *the love of God*.

There are forty-two kings of Israel and Judah in the Old Testament—only one of them is described as the man after God's own heart (1 Samuel 13:14). Would you like that to be the chief description of your life? *A man or woman after God's own heart.* If so, something fundamental must be understood: You cannot resemble that which you do not know. You cannot find consolation in a subject that is foreign to you. Therefore, David meditated on the heart of God and basked in the reality of God's love for him. David's Excalibur against worry and anxiety was not only God's rule and reign but His faithful love and care. The revelation of God's love for David propelled him to praise the Lord amid his flight from Saul and say, "I love you, O LORD, my strength. The LORD is my rock and my fortress and my deliverer, my God, my rock, in whom I take refuge" (Psalm 18:1–2 ESV).

What Is Love?

Perhaps no word in the English language has been stripped and starved of its meaning more than the word *love*. We say "I love you" to our family and say "I loved it" about our meal at Taco Bell. This variance in meaning and application has not only affected our modern vernacular but has contributed to the way we view God's love for His children. God's love, which is His most well-known attribute, is likely the least understood in our world and in the contemporary church today. It may also be the hardest truth to believe when we experience pain and are afflicted by anxiety. Many people would sooner doubt God's love than they would His control. It's not hard for me to believe that God rules and reigns over everything He has made. It is much more difficult, however, to believe in God's love for me when I am in great pain.[2] And yet the Bible details that God's love is a source of great hope and sure comfort for those who are worn down by worry and despair.

God's Holy Love

Perhaps there is no better way to understand God's love than to conjoin His love to His holiness. As I have already mentioned, when we are examining one attribute of God, we cannot demarcate one attribute from another or separate the part from the whole. Remember, God's attributes are not like slices of a pie. He is, in theological terms, *simple*, not simplistic, but simple in the sense that He is not composed of parts. Therefore, as we survey the wondrous love of God, we must remember: *His love is holy*. Sadly, you can grow up singing "holy, holy, holy" and never respond like Isaiah when he heard the seraphim proclaiming these very words. When we want to emphasize something in our writing, we often highlight, circle, or underline, but when God wants to reinforce a reality within the revelation that He has given to us in His Word, He repeats it. And in Scripture there is only one attribute of God that is elevated to this superlative degree, and that is God's holiness.[3]

The question is asked in Exodus 15:11, "Who is like you, O Lord . . . majestic in holiness?" (ESV).

What's the answer?

No one.

God never points outside Himself to define Himself because there is nothing and no one like Him. And more than any other attribute, God is identified by His own holiness. You may be wondering, *What does this have to do with God's love?* The answer: everything.

I remember seeing a man wearing a shirt with the words "Jesus is my homeboy" across the front—I can only assume he had the intention of exhibiting his relationship with Jesus. But in a spirit of good intentions, I believe the man was incorrect in his application of biblical truth. If you're in Christ, God *is* your Friend, He *is* your Father, He *is* your Savior, but it must not be forgotten: He is also the King of creation. And because God is holy, no one fist-bumps God. He is an exalted King, not our next-door neighbor. We do enter His presence *boldly* because of the blood of Christ, but we do not come to Him *flippantly* or *cavalierly* (Hebrews 4:16).

In an attempt to elevate the love of God, our contemporary church culture has, for all practical purposes, denied the truth of His holiness. In doing so, they understand neither. Perhaps the people who have the most difficult time experiencing God's love are those who grew up singing, "Amazing love! How can it be that Thou, my God, shouldst die for me?" Why? Because love is only "amazing" to those who don't think they deserve it—and the only way you will come to grips with your unworthiness of God's love is when you begin to comprehend His holiness.

Because God is holy, His "eyes are too pure to look on evil" (Habakkuk 1:13 NIV), He takes no pleasure in wickedness (Psalm 5:4), and His just judgment must be poured out on all sin. God abhors sin. It is an assault to His holiness. You may be still wondering, *What does this have to do with God's love?* Namely this: You cannot understand God's love until you understand what He hates—God hates sin. Right views of God's holiness always precede right views of His love. God's holiness speaks not only of His moral purity but to His total otherness. His transcendence. His majesty. His entire being is *other*. The more we understand who He is as a holy king, the more we can, even remotely, begin to fathom His love.

I remember hearing Sinclair Ferguson say this:

The greater the lover, the greater the love.
The lesser the object of love, the greater the giver of love.
The greater the demonstration of love, the more marvelous
that love truly is.

As we consider God's love, we must (1) magnify our view of
the Lover and (2) lessen our view of ourselves so that we can more
appropriately (3) behold and fathom the demonstration of God's
love for us in Christ. People often forget (or were never taught)
that they were not born children of God but born *children of wrath*
(Ephesians 2). We were not born friends of God, we were born His
enemies (Romans 5:8–10). We were not born citizens of heaven
but citizens *of the domain of darkness* (Colossians 1:13–14). When
we lose sight of this, we will inevitably lose sight of and comfort
in God's love. There was nothing in us that wooed the heart of
God. There was nothing in us that caught His eye. Contemporary
church culture preaches slogans such as "You are lovable," and
while this is true, it is not because of who we are but because of
who we are in Christ. Sentimental, seeker-sensitive, and shallow
teaching on the love of God has rendered it powerless in the real
battle we wage against the adversary of our souls and the afflictions we face in our lives. So we must start here, but we must not
stop. Because the first feature of God's love makes the second all
the more amazing.

God's Forgiving Love

In Psalm 103, David said, "Bless the LORD, O my soul, and forget not all his benefits" (v. 2 ESV) and then goes on to recount the

greatest benefit we could ever receive from God by adding, "who forgives all your sins" (v. 3 NIV).

Dear reader, how many of your sins has God forgiven you if you're in Christ?

All of them.

My friend Erik Thoennes once put it this way: "Satan wins if you believe God has forgiven you of 99.9 percent of your sin."[4] Do you believe that God has forgiven you of your sin, *except for that one thing in your past?* If you're in Christ, God forgives *all* your sin, and not only that—He also removes your sin.

How far?

"As far as the east is from the west, so far has He removed our transgressions from us" (Psalm 103:12). An infinite distance by an infinitely loving God. You cannot look in two directions at once, and when God looks at you in Christ, He no longer sees your sin. He has plunged your sin into the deepest corner of the deepest ocean. Our doubts that God has forgiven us of our sin will inevitably lead to anxiety. After all, how could we have the peace *of* God if we aren't sure we are at peace *with* God? Our confidence in this area of God's love is the surest catalyst to peace—regardless of life's circumstances! If God has already met our greatest need in life by forgiving our sin, won't He also richly supply all our other needs in Christ Jesus? If He did not spare His only Son, will He not also give us all things (Romans 8:32)? There is no more for heaven to give!

Are you anxious because you lack the assurance that God has forgiven you of all your sin? Do you lack the peace *of* God because you dwell so little on the wondrous reality that you are at peace *with* God through the work of Jesus Christ? Every believer has been positionally made right with God, but when believers sin (and we all do), we need to come again to the fountain of God's mercy, not to be saved all over again, but so that Christ might cleanse us from sin and purify our consciences (1 John 1:9). David said that when he kept silent about his sin, he felt as if his bones were breaking and his life's vitality was draining away (Psalm 32:3–4 NIV). If you are a Christian, your conscience will condemn you when you run from God, reject His Word, and rebel against His will. Harboring sin is an exhausting weight that crushes our souls—and anxiety is the inevitable offspring of a repeatedly violated conscience. But there is no rest, no peace, and no joy that is quite like that which comes from falling on the mercy of Christ and receiving cleansing, not just of our sin but of our dirtied consciences (Hebrews 9:14). Isn't it amazing? Our Father knows the worst about us, and He loves us the most. His forgiveness is offered to the deepest and darkest corners of our hearts. He not only forgives, but He loves to do so. *Oh, how blessed is the man whose sin is forgiven!*[5]

God's Satisfying Love

In Scripture, God's love is not merely an objective fact that needs to be notionally affirmed but a marvelous truth that must be subjectively experienced. David said in Psalm 63:3, "Because Your lovingkindness is better than life, my lips shall praise You" (NKJV). According to David, God's love is so real and so satisfying that it is "better than life." John Piper said, "Every true Christian knows the love of God not just as an argument, but as an experience."[6] Similarly, David didn't say to "believe and affirm that God is good," he said to "taste and see" (Psalm 34:8). Have you tasted and experienced God's love? We occasionally live vicariously through other people's vacations, homes, and experiences and then dream as if they were our own—but experiencing God's love cannot be done by proxy. It must be experienced *personally*. Can I give you an example? You could have your PhD in food science and understand the molecular complexity of every gram, but if you do not taste food for yourself, you will starve and die. Conversely, you may not know the macro-nutrients of a meal, you may be ignorant of its ingredients, but after tasting that meal, you can declare, "This is wonderful!" The same thing is true of God's love. You can be a first-time reader of Scripture and read "God so loved the world" (John 3:16) and cry out within your heart, *Oh, how marvelous, how wonderful is my Savior's love for me!* Contrarily, you could affirm the truth of God's matchless love and analyze the subject in the original languages, yet never sense the wonder of it in your heart.

God's love is indeed demonstrated to the world, and yet His love is immensely personal—one of the chief functions of the Holy Spirit is to pour the love of God into our hearts (Romans 5:5). Isn't this wonderful? God's love is not divided among His infinite number of children; rather, His infinite love is extended toward His children individually so that they might be satisfied by His love "all our days" (Psalm 90:14).

God's Loyal Love

In the year 586 BC the prophet Jeremiah began writing the short book of Lamentations—wherein he *lamented* the destruction of Jerusalem. The people had been killed, the city had been destroyed, and the Babylonians had prevailed. But amid the chaos, heartbreak, and confusion, "the weeping prophet" Jeremiah wrote some of the sweetest words in all of Scripture:

> Remember my misery and my homelessness, the
> wormwood and bitterness.
> My soul certainly remembers,
> And is bent over within me.
> I recall this to my mind,

> Therefore I wait.
> The Lord's acts of mercy indeed do not end,
> For His compassions do not fail.
> They are new every morning;
> Great is Your faithfulness.
> "The Lord is my portion," says my soul,
> "Therefore I wait for Him." (Lamentations 3:19–24 NASB 2020)

Man's love is fickle. It is often unfaithful. But God's love is *loyal*, His lovingkindness *never ceases*, and *His compassions never fail*. Perhaps no word carries with it more significance in the Hebrew Old Testament than the word *hesed*. This word is often translated "lovingkindness" or "steadfast love" and it refers to God's patient, enduring, compassionate, kind, and loyal love. God's *hesed* love is a love that will not let you go. A summary of the book of Lamentations would be "Life is hard, God is good. Pain is real. So is God's love. This world will come to an end, but God's love will not."

Christian, are you anxious about forfeiting the love of God? You can't. God's love is loyal, it is faithful, His compassions never fail, and neither does His love.

God's Fatherly Love

Psalm 103:13 says, "Just as a father has compassion on his children, so the Lord has compassion on those who fear Him." Did you know that nearly every chapter in the Quran begins with the words *Allah, the merciful and compassionate*? The problem is that the Allah revealed in the Quran is not merciful or compassionate at all. He grades people based on their performance, not according to grace. Even Islam's greatest prophet, Mohammed, had no assurance of his standing before Allah (Quran 46:9). Why? Because the Quran presents Allah as a distant judge, not a loving and compassionate father. A few years ago, I was preaching in a predominantly Islamic country on how God is a loving Father to those who come to Him—that He not only rescues His enemies and forgives them of all their sin but also adopts them as His sons and daughters. Afterward, a boy came up to me and grabbed me on the shoulders and said, "How come no one has ever told me there was a God of love? Allah never loved me." I'll never forget it. The truth that many have become so accustomed to hearing is the reality that shook a young teenager to his core. Do you believe this? Your heavenly Father loves you.

Isaiah 49:15–16 says, "Can a woman forget her nursing child and have no compassion on the son of her womb? Even these may forget, but I will not forget you. Behold, I have inscribed you on the palms of My hands." The idea of my wife forgetting either of our precious daughters is unthinkable. Why? We love them. We understand parental love on a human level, but every earthly father's love pales in comparison to our heavenly Father's love for His own. We are not abandoned and unloved, we are adopted and cherished through Jesus Christ. Martyn Lloyd-Jones used to say that the moment we understand God's fatherly love, everything else will soon change. Is that the case for you? Has God's fatherly love changed everything? Paul said in Romans that we are no longer slaves but sons and daughters—we have received the spirit of adoption that cries out, "Abba! Father!" (Romans 8:15).

Do you doubt that God could love you? Well, in one sense, that would be true if God's love was a derivative of your performance. But the truth of Scripture teaches us that God's love is not extended on the basis of our merits, backgrounds, pedigree, knowledge, usefulness, gifts, or experiences—we are loved for one main reason: God's matchless mercy and grace. And His love is received by all who come to Him in faith. Pay attention to the words of John's Gospel: "But as many as received Him, to them He gave the right to become *children of God*, even to those who believe in His name" (John 1:12, emphasis added). Our adoption is based not on our worthiness but on our Father's kindness. It's amazing, yet nonetheless true—your heavenly Father truly does love you. Therefore, worry is an insult both to God's sovereignty and to His love. When we worry, we say, *Father, You do not really love me, and You are not really in control.* Set your mind and fix your gaze on this reality: *I am loved by my heavenly Father.* A failure to meditate on God's love will starve you of peace, but not only that—a failure to abide in God's love *is a sin.* Have you ever thought about that? Jesus said, "Abide in my love" (John 15:9 ESV)—that's not a suggestion, that's a commandment that we are privileged to obey. In considering our Father's love, we can say with Scripture, "Perfect love casts out fear" (1 John 4:18 ESV).

God's Everlasting Love

In the parched Palestinian climate, the dew functions as the father for tiny sprouts of grass that spring up in the early morning. These sprouts shoot up fast, but their life is very brief. The hot sun scorches the grass before they have time to see their first sunset. And Scripture repeatedly emphasizes that man is like grass. Charles Spurgeon said, "Here is the history of grass—sown, grown, blown, mown, gone."[7] Job said our days are "swifter than a weaver's shuttle" (Job 7:6). Solomon said, "Vanity of vanities. . . . All is vanity" (Ecclesiastes 1:2 ESV). James said, "You do not know what your life will be like tomorrow" (James 4:14). Our lives are far more fleeting and temporary than we like to think. But the truth of Scripture is *grass withers, flowers fade,* and men are transient, but God's love "is from everlasting to everlasting" (Psalm 103:17). Do you believe this? God's love for you had no beginning, and it will never have an end—His love is *everlasting*. Jesus said, "I give eternal life to them, and they will never perish; and no one will snatch them out of My hand" (John 10:28). All the demons of hell and Satan himself cannot pluck a single child of God out of our Father's hand. He loved us "before the foundation of the world" (Ephesians 1:4) and He will love us for all eternity. What does God's everlasting love tell us? It tells us this: that if His love for His children is from everlasting to everlasting, then you can be sure that His love is not dependent on human performance. He loved you before time began, and He will love you when time is over.

God's Love Is Demonstrated in Christ

God's love is not a hypothetical or theoretical abstract idea, it is a historical, objective, and demonstrated reality. God tells His people plainly in Scripture that He loves them. Jeremiah 31:3 reads, "I have loved you with an everlasting love." But God does more than declare His love; He demonstrates His love toward us in the person and work of Jesus Christ.

I love the language in Titus 3:4–7:

> But when the kindness of God our Savior and His love for man-kind appeared, He saved us, not on the basis of deeds which we have done in righteousness, but according to His mercy, by the washing of regeneration and renewing by the Holy Spirit, whom He poured out upon us richly through Jesus Christ our Savior, so that being justified by His grace we would be made heirs according to the hope of eternal life.

You may need to read that first verse again. Paul said that God's kindness and His love "appeared." Astonishing. God's love is not a distant illusion that His followers cling onto amid their despair, but rather His love "appeared" in the incarnation when "the Word [Jesus] became flesh, and dwelt among us" (John 1:14). There is never any distinction between what God *says* and what He *does*. He not only proclaims His love, but He proves it most clearly in the work of Jesus Christ.

We have previously examined the sovereignty of God and what was mentioned then and must be reiterated now is that God's sovereignty is always tethered to His love. Paul reminds us in Galatians of the twin truths of God's sovereignty and demonstrated love when he wrote, "But when the fullness of the time came, God sent forth His Son, born of a woman, born under the Law, so that He might redeem those who were under the Law, that we might receive the adoption as sons" (Galatians 4:4–5). In His perfect sovereignty, Christ's love "appeared" neither a moment too soon nor a moment too late, but "when the fullness of the time" had come.

We previously examined God's forgiving love, but the question we must consider now is this: *How can a holy and righteous God pardon sins?*

He cannot.

Sin must be punished.

Therefore, in a true sense, God *always* punishes sin. That is why Jesus came to die (1 Timothy 1:15). You simply cannot understand God's love until you understand His justice. Why? Because the greatest demonstration of God's love is in the pouring out of His wrath on His only beloved Son.

Something must be done about sin! It cannot be left unpunished! Jesus said, "I will bear it."

In Gethsemane, Jesus prayed, "Father, if You are willing, remove this cup from Me; yet not My will, but Yours be done" (Luke 22:42). But to what cup did Jesus refer? The cup of God's wrath and justice toward sin. After all, *what did Christ come to save us from?* Romans 5:9 tells us, "Much more then, having now been justified by His blood, we shall be saved *from the wrath of God* through Him" (emphasis added). The marvel of the gospel is that God has placed your sins upon Christ and "the chastisement for our well-being *fell* upon Him" (Isaiah 53:5, emphasis added). Every lustful thought, glance, and deed; every angry, gossiping, and slanderous word; every dishonest, unkind, and hypocritical action was placed on Jesus Christ. On the cross, God declared Jesus legally guilty of every sin ever committed by everyone who would ever believe—and then He poured out the full cup of His wrath on Jesus, who drank it for us "down to the dregs" (Psalm 75:8 ESV). Have you found comfort and peace in this reality? There is not a single drop left in the cup of God's wrath toward you because you are in Christ Jesus—and *Jesus paid it all.* God has taken your sin, but not only that—He has transferred over to you the spotless, sinless, and blameless life of His only Son (2 Corinthians 5:21). Right now, God views you as righteous, not because of the righteousness you *produce,* but because of the righteousness you *possess* in Christ Jesus.

Do you doubt this love?

Anxiety is inevitable if we do not believe God loves us. God's love is not a figment of our imagination—His love was demonstrated at the cross of Calvary and has been poured out into our hearts through His Holy Spirit (Romans 5:5).

God's Transforming Love

At this point you may be wondering: *If God loves me so much, why do I experience so much pain, affliction, and despair?* The answer is simple, yet not always easy to swallow—God loves to transform those whom He loves. God bids us to come to Him as we are, but He loves us too much to let us remain the same. Every ounce of affliction and pain in our lives is superintended and sovereignly orchestrated by a God who has a plan for His glory and for our transformation into the image of His Son.

Knowing God's Love

Jesus' final recorded prayer, in John 17, is called the High Priestly Prayer. It's one of the most breathtaking chapters in the Bible. Jesus was praying to the Father before His betrayal, and the disciples were listening in as Jesus communed with His Father. Do you know what was the very last thing Jesus prayed for before His arrest? Jesus prayed, "I in them and You in Me, that they may be perfected in unity, so that the world may know that You sent Me, and loved them, even as You have loved Me" (John 17:23). Read those words again. How much does the Father love you? *As much as the Father loves His only Son, Jesus Christ.* Can you bear the thought? Jesus then prayed that His redeemed would come to "know" this love—not in an academic sense, but in an intimate one.

Remember, you are the sum of your thoughts of God. No one's religion ever ascends higher than who he or she believes God to be. And if you can think of your heavenly Father and possess a small regard for His love, then the most important thing about you—your view of God—is flawed. But if you come to God's Word and receive His wondrous love, then you can rejoice with Paul and say:

> Who will separate us from the love of Christ? Will tribulation, or distress, or persecution, or famine, or nakedness, or peril, or sword? . . . But in all these things we overwhelmingly conquer through Him who loved us. For I am convinced that neither death, nor life, nor angels, nor principalities, nor things present, nor things to come, nor powers, nor height, nor depth, nor any

other created thing will be able to separate us from the love of God, which is in Christ Jesus our Lord. (Romans 8:35–39)

————— **Reflection Questions** —————

1. Read John 17:23. Have you ever thought about how Jesus prayed that *you* would know His love more deeply? What response should that invoke from us as His own? What are ways you can abide in His love?

2. Read Lamentations 3:19–24. Why does God's loyal love give Jeremiah hope during difficult days?

3. Read Romans 8:35–39. What can separate you from God's love? How can you set your hope and fix your gaze on this reality?

CHAPTER 11

Our Present Refuge

In recent years we've witnessed pandemics, elections, murder hornets (yes, you read that correctly), faltering supply chains, weakening borders, soaring gas prices, and global instability. In the past year I have waded through reports that read "US and China Tension Grows," "Earthquake in Turkey and Syria Kills 60,000," "Russia Invades Ukraine," "Iran Strengthens Nuclear Arsenal," "World War III Looms," and last year, in my own city, the newspaper read: "School Shooting Kills Six."

And these are just the headlines.

But behind the news stories are *our* stories. Stories of cancer, layoffs, breakups, loneliness, miscarriages, and infertility. Stories that cause us to consider the confusion, madness, and mayhem of the world in which we live. Our hearts and minds are inclined toward worry and fear. Both the children of God and the children of this world read the same headlines—they both feel the effects of living as fallen creatures in a fallen world—but only a Christian can anchor in the precious promise that we will examine in this chapter. Each new day brings new headlines that remind us of the instability and uncertainty in our world. Thankfully, even though the news coverage spouts current events, current situations, and current catastrophes, the truth of Scripture says, "There is nothing *new* under the sun" (Ecclesiastes 1:9, emphasis added)—the worries we face *today* are the worries God addresses in Scripture.

Hezekiah's Trouble

Eleven of the psalms are attributed to the sons of Korah—one of which is Psalm 46. As is the case with other passages in Scripture's hymnal, this psalm is historically rooted in the life of God's people at a time when they faced real physical danger and psychological fear. Facing insurmountable odds, King Hezekiah and the entire city of Jerusalem were compelled to ask: *Can we really trust God?*

The year was 701 BC. Sennacherib's mighty Assyrian army had conquered every neighboring nation in its path. The reports of their ruthlessness and dominance had reached the people of God, and, before long, Sennacherib's army of more than two hundred thousand men gathered outside the city walls of Jerusalem while the people of God quaked with fear within. In 2 Kings 18, the commander of Sennacherib's army mocked, derided, and intimidated those within the city by proclaiming:

> "Do not let Hezekiah deceive you, for he will not be able to deliver you from my hand, nor let Hezekiah make you trust in the LORD, saying, 'The LORD will surely deliver us, and this city will not be given into the hand of the king of Assyria.' ... Has any one of the gods of the nations delivered his land from the hand of the king of Assyria? ... Who among all the gods of the lands have delivered their land from my hand, that the LORD should deliver Jerusalem from my hand?" (2 Kings 18:29–30, 33, 35)

Hezekiah, the king of Judah, heard the jeers from Sennacherib's army and was seized with fear. Wouldn't you be? In response to the Assyrian's taunts, Hezekiah tore his clothes, covered his head with sackcloth, fell on his knees, and prayed:

> O LORD, the God of Israel, who are enthroned above the cherubim, You are the God, You alone, of all the kingdoms of the earth. You have made heaven and earth. Incline Your ear, O LORD, and hear; open Your eyes, O LORD, and see; and listen to the words of Sennacherib, which he has sent to reproach the living God. Truly, O LORD, the kings of Assyria have devastated the nations and their lands and have cast their gods into the fire, for they were not gods but the work of men's hands, wood and stone. So they have destroyed them. Now, O LORD our God, I pray, deliver us from his hand that all the kingdoms of the earth may know that You alone, O LORD, are God. (2 Kings 19:15–19)

How does the story end?

> Then it happened that night that the angel of the LORD went out and struck 185,000 in the camp of the Assyrians; and when the men rose early in the morning, behold, all of them were dead. So Sennacherib king of Assyria departed and returned home, and lived at Nineveh. It came about as he was worshiping in the house of Nisroch his god, that Adrammelech and Sharezer killed him with the sword; and they escaped into the land of Ararat. And Esarhaddon his son became king in his place. (2 Kings 19:35–37)

God Is Our Refuge

Powerful songs come from powerful stories. And it is against this backdrop that the sons of Korah penned Psalm 46 as they rejoiced in God's power and deliverance. The opening verse reads, "God is our refuge and strength, a very present help in trouble" (ESV). In the Bible, even verb tenses are inspired by God and are worth noting. The psalm does not say, "God *was* our refuge and strength," nor does it say, "God *will be* our refuge and strength," but "God *is* our refuge and strength." What Scripture declares *then* is true of God *now*. He has never increased in power and will never decrease in power. He will never be more or less present for His people as He was 2,700 years ago during the reign of Hezekiah. The Christian's great comfort amid great distress is that God *is* our refuge.

A refuge is a shelter that protects you from danger; it is a stronghold that keeps you safe. And the psalmist details that when the people of God have nowhere else to turn, when enemies or trouble is encroaching in, when it seems as if all hope is lost, God is your refuge. This is one of the predominant distinctions between a child of God and a child of this world: only the Christian *always* has a place to go.[1] Whether we are facing little skirmishes or big battles in our lives, we must turn to God. David said in Psalm 62:8, "Trust in Him at all times, O people; pour out your hearts before Him; God is a refuge for us." There are so many moments in our lives when we must pour out our hearts before Him, and it is our great comfort that in those moments the gates to the refuge of our heavenly Father are never shut; His help is ever present.

God Is Our Strength

Weary and worried souls need refuge from the gusts and gales of this life, but not only that—they need strength. In Psalm 42, the sons of Korah put words to the experience of God's children throughout the centuries: "My tears have been my food day and night, while they say to me all day long, 'Where is your God?' . . . Why are you in despair,

O my soul? And why have you become disturbed within me?" (vv. 3, 5). Despairing and downcast children of God must flee to God's supernatural shelter of peace, but very few come walking without a limp. Fainthearted souls need to be strengthened. Therefore, the psalmist says in Psalm 46:1 that God is not only "our refuge," but He is also "our strength." In a troubled and tempestuous world, God not only protects the fearful; He also strengthens and energizes the downcast. The Christian life is not hard, it's impossible—you cannot live it in your own strength. Therefore, we need God to give us what we cannot give ourselves. The Christian faith is not the story of a lot of strong men and strong women; it's the story of the weak whom God makes strong through His power. Paul said, "When I am weak, then I am strong" (2 Corinthians 12:10).

When I was growing up, I used to hear people say things like "That man is a strong believer." In most ways, I understand what they meant. But being a Christian isn't machismo, it's the humble recognition that even on your strongest day you are too weak to live for God, without God. At times, God must deplete us physically and emotionally of all strength so that we would be compelled to find our strength in Him. Perhaps Paul would have never learned to acknowledge that God's grace is sufficient for him (2 Corinthians 12:9) unless he had first learned, through means of the thorn in his flesh, that his own strength was indeed insufficient. Only when we come to the end of our own strength will we be able to say with the psalmist, "The LORD is my strength and my shield; my heart trusts in him, and he helps me" (Psalm 28:7 NIV).

Papier-Mâché Refuges

We live in a world of trouble and pain, and the truth is we are hardwired to seek shelter from it. Yet we often run to the things and people of this world as our stronghold instead of to our heavenly Father. People place their trust in pensions, passive income, and portfolios rather than in God Himself. They seek strongholds in treasures and securities here on earth instead of in the God who sits on the throne of heaven. The Bible never condemns money itself, but it does compel us to consider whether money can become a false refuge.

As a nation or as individuals we may look to economic, political, or military power as a refuge, and when all else fails, we call on God. We use God as a divine cop-out and as a divine 911. Instead of our Father being our first call in the moment of trouble, He becomes our last resort. Those who run to papier-mâché refuges and popsicle-stick strongholds can never say with David, "The LORD is my rock and my fortress and my deliverer, my God, my rock, in whom I take refuge; my shield and the horn of my salvation, my stronghold" (Psalm 18:2). It is indeed human nature to put our trust in human resources and human instruments, but the Christian must learn to run to God.

Are you facing a battle right now in your life?

Is there something that overwhelms you?

Is there a sleep-stealing thing that keeps you awake at night?

A trial, a temptation, a trouble?

Do you feel drained, weary, despairing, and despondent?

Then can I just ask you as I have at times asked myself: Is it possible that part of your problem is that you're trying to cope with your trouble in your own strength? Could it be that you aren't running to God as a refuge and relying on Him as your strength? Let the words of Isaiah comfort you even now: "He gives strength to the weary and increases the power of the weak. Even youths grow tired and weary, and young men stumble and fall; but those who hope in the LORD will renew their strength. They will soar on wings like eagles; they will run and not grow weary; they will walk and not be faint" (Isaiah 40:29–31 NIV). We are not strong in our power;

therefore, Paul exhorted the Ephesian church to "be strong in the Lord and in his mighty power" (Ephesians 6:10 NIV).

God Is with Us

Ancient strongholds were typically in elevated positions. Those who were in the lowlands would emerge from their homes when neighboring nations attacked and would flee to the refuge. On the journey, they could be overcome and ambushed, and there was the fear of never making it to the refuge at all. Fleeing to a place of protection was a risk in itself. Why? Because the refuge was *distant*. It was a far way off.

But what does the Bible say about our God?

Is He a distant refuge?

No, the psalmist said that our Father is an "ever-present help in trouble" (Psalm 46:1 NIV). The literal rendering of this in Hebrew is that God is *a very findable refuge*. You don't have to travel to find Him. He is as near as your next breath, and He is nearer than your trouble itself.

Every story has a storyline, and one of the great storylines of Scripture is that God is not a distant deity; He is near to those who run to Him. Furthermore, He never takes a leave of absence. He is not a "sometimes-present God," nor is He an "often-present God"—He is an "ever-present help in trouble." Theologians refer to the great truth of God's presence as *omnipresence*, speaking to the reality that God is everywhere. He sees all, knows all, and is *always* with His people. God's transcendence speaks to the reality that He is lofty, independent of created matter, and gloriously exalted in His heavenly home—He is, in other words, *holy*. But, amazingly, our lofty, exalted, and transcendent God is also *immanent*—which means that He is near.

In Psalm 139:7–12 (NIV), David, who was often anxious, lonely, fearful, and despairing, buttressed his own soul with the profound truth of God's nearness:

> Where can I go from your Spirit?
> Where can I flee from your presence?
> If I go up to the heavens, you are there;
> if I make my bed in the depths, you are there.
> If I rise on the wings of the dawn,
> if I settle on the far side of the sea,
> even there your hand will guide me,
> your right hand will hold me fast.
> If I say, "Surely the darkness will hide me
> and the light become night around me,"
> even the darkness will not be dark to you;
> the night will shine like the day,
> for darkness is as light to you.

Those who are running from God are horrified by His all-pervasive nearness, but to those who love God, this precious truth brings indescribable peace. In Psalm 139, David was reflecting on the fact that whether he went north, south, east, or west, God was with him—not because God follows us where we are going, but because wherever we go, *God is already there*. There is not one place on earth where God is more available or more present than another place. He is always equally present and available to help those who come to Him. At times it may seem as though God is a far way off (Psalm 13:1), but the truth of God's Word is that He is "near to all who call upon Him" (Psalm 145:18). God's promise to His children is "I will never leave you nor forsake you" (Hebrews 13:5 ESV). This brings both great comfort and great courage to those who walk along the highways and byways of this life. Our God never leaves us. He never looks the other way. He is never hard to find. He is always near.

Lord of Hosts

So that we do not minimize the magnitude of God's nearness in our lives, God reminds His children in Psalm 46 of the gravity and strength of the One who is with us: "The LORD of hosts is with us" (vv. 7, 11 ESV). This phrase, *adonai tzva'ot*, which is translated "Lord of Hosts" or "Lord of armies," is used approximately 250 times in the Bible. Now, considering the context of this psalm, think with me: one angel in 2 Kings 19 wiped out 185,000 Assyrians, and yet God is the Lord of Hosts. Your Father is the general of angel armies. He is a warrior. And He is with you.

We see a glimpse of this reality in 2 Kings 6. The city of Dothan had been surrounded by the armies of Ben-hadad in an attempt to capture Elisha. Elisha's servant saw the army surrounding the city and ran in fear to Elisha and said, "Oh, my lord, what shall we do?" (v. 15 NCB). Elisha responded: "Do not fear, for those who are with us are more than those who are with them" (v. 16 NKJV). Then Elisha prayed, "'O LORD, I pray, open his eyes that he may see.' And the LORD opened the servant's eyes and he saw; and behold, the mountain was full of horses and chariots of fire all around Elisha" (v. 17).

God's children do not possess a junior-varsity aid; we possess the commander of angelic armies and the King over all creation. The level of comfort and courage that God's presence brings to our minds is in direct proportion to the power, majesty, and authority we ascribe to Him. The strongest weapons raised against Him are mere squirt guns to the Lord of Hosts. We must put on the armor of God, for we need protection in this life from the devil, the world, and our sinful flesh, but we take confidence in this: the battle is already won. When we "take up the shield of faith" (Ephesians 6:16 ESV), we are, by God's grace, employing the defense that can come only from Him. In your loneliest moment, in your weakest position, in your most fearful stage, God is as near as your next breath. He is the one who gives strength to the weary and He is the one who will never leave you or forsake you. What a wonderful thing it is to be a child of God! The world is without a true refuge, without supernatural strength, and in need of constant help in this life. But God is with us! Therefore, God tells us in His Word to "cast your burden upon the LORD and He will sustain you; He will never allow the righteous to be shaken" (Psalm 55:22).

Be Anxious for Nothing

All great truths about God should produce appropriate responses from His people. Psalm 46:1 reads, "God is our refuge and strength, an ever-present help in trouble" (NIV). What is our response? Psalm 46 goes on to say in verses 2 and 3, "Therefore we will not fear, though the earth should change and though the mountains slip into the heart of the sea; though its waters roar and foam, though the mountains quake at its swelling pride." In a world of chaos, the believer does not panic. Why? Because God is near.

Martyn Lloyd-Jones used to say, "Faith is the refusal to panic."[2] Why? Because there is no panic in heaven, only plans. The psalmist was begging us to ask, *What reason could we possibly have to be worried when the God of angel armies is with us and is a constant refuge for His people?* The psalm states that even if "the mountains slip into the heart of the sea," if everything should change and foreign armies invade, if hostility comes, the economy crashes, our nest egg is crushed, our talents disappear, or our scholarships are taken away, we will not fear, because God is our refuge.

Consider the Lilies

Is God your refuge? The Christian's refuge is not God plus something or someone else—our refuge is God, and God alone.

Paul said, "Be anxious for nothing, but in everything by prayer and supplication, with thanksgiving, let your requests be made known to God; and the peace of God, which surpasses all understanding, will guard your hearts and minds through Christ Jesus." These words from Philippians 4:6–7 (NKJV) are likely familiar to you at this point, but what may be unfamiliar to you is the truth in verse 5, which provides the basis for our peace: "The Lord is near."

Why should there be an absence of anxiety in our lives? Because of the nearness of God.

The earth may quake and shake, but God is the Rock of Ages.

The earth may change, but "I, the Lord, do not change" (Malachi 3:6).

The world can be in flames, yet we are within the refuge that is God, nourished by His supply and comforted by His presence. This is not to say that there will be no persecution, affliction, trouble, or pain for God's people (because those are promised realities), but to say that, in the midst of it, God is building His church, preserving His own, and comforting His people.

Be Still and Know

Psalm 46 concludes with these well-known words: "Be still, and know that I am God. I will be exalted among the nations, I will be exalted in the earth!" The Lord of hosts is with us; the God of Jacob is our fortress" (vv. 10–11 ESV). Are you going through something right now? Is your health failing? Are your relationships breaking? Is your financial future deteriorating? Sometimes, when life's circumstances are tempestuous, we say that our lives are "falling apart." At times life can be likened to the imagery we see in

Psalm 46—mountains are tumbling, the earth is tottering—yet it is a powerful comfort to know that in the hurly-burly of all that is shaken, one thing is not: God is not shaken.[3]

Verses that are most well-known are often the most misunderstood. And such is the case when we come to the second-to-last verse of Psalm 46. "Be still, and know that I am God" (v. 10 NIV) is not the call for us to live quiet or meditative lives; it's not merely the verse you put as an Instagram caption as you drink your coffee by a calm summer lake; it's a truth that draws us toward something—Someone—much bigger. The command to "be still" is against the backdrop of the quaking earth (v. 2), raging sea (v. 3), and warring nations (v. 9), and, exalted above the madness, lifted high above the mayhem, is a God who thunderously says, "Quiet! Be still! Know that I am God!" Our call to "stop striving" is a call to surrender all claims of control and to fall down in worship before a God who is a sturdy refuge to His people. The call for *stillness* is a call for *submission* to the Rock of Ages.

It was in reflecting on the words of this very psalm that Martin Luther was prompted to pen the hymn "A Mighty Fortress":

> A mighty fortress is our God, a bulwark never
> failing;
> our helper He, amid the flood of mortal ills
> prevailing.
> For still our ancient foe does seek to work us woe;
> his craft and power are great, and armed with cruel hate,
> on earth is not his equal.
> Did we in our own strength confide, our striving
> would be losing,
> were not the right Man on our side, the Man of
> God's own choosing.
> You ask who that may be? Christ Jesus, it is He;

Lord Sabaoth His name, from age to age the same;
and He must win the battle.
And though this world, with devils filled, should
    threaten to undo us,
we will not fear, for God has willed His truth to
    triumph through us.
The prince of darkness grim, we tremble not for him;
his rage we can endure, for lo! his doom is sure;
one little word shall fell him.
That Word above all earthly powers no thanks to
    them abideth;
the Spirit and the gifts are ours through Him who
    with us sideth.
Let goods and kindred go, this mortal life also;
the body they may kill: God's truth abideth still;
His kingdom is forever!

—————— Reflection Questions ——————

1. Read Psalm 46:1–3. What is the psalmist's response to God's strength? How might God's nearness contribute to our peace? What does it mean to "be still"?

2. Read 2 Corinthians 12:9. How did Paul's weaknesses and insufficiency allow him to experience and learn the strength and sufficiency of God?

3. Read Philippians 4:4–6. What is Scripture's exhortation toward our worry and anxiety? Why is meditating on God's nearness a prerequisite to living a life of peace?

CHAPTER 12

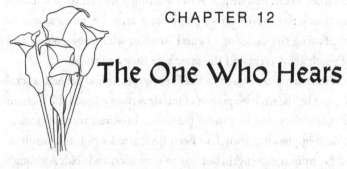

The One Who Hears

A s I've mentioned, I'm a reader. And one of my favorite genres of literature is historical biography. I recently read a biography of Napoleon Bonaparte—who is known as a gifted leader, skilled politician, and, more than anything else, a brilliant military strategist. As famous as Napoleon is for his military feats, however, he is also famous for his catastrophic faults. In 1812, Napoleon's Grande Armée had grown to the staggering size of six hundred thousand men. With the unprecedented size of his army, Napoleon seized unprecedented control. But Napoleon was not satisfied with the immensity of his empire; he was determined to control an even larger territory and further cement his legacy. Napoleon had set his eyes on Russia.

After crossing the Neman River and entering Russian territory, Napoleon found himself warring against a Russian army in perpetual retreat. The Russian general, knowing that he could not contend with Napoleon's massive army in a head-to-head confrontation, employed a tactic known as attrition warfare, wherein you attempt to grind down your enemy's ability to wage war by forcing them to exhaust all their energy, resources, and supplies.

On September 7, the indecisive Battle of Borodino was fought, and on September 14, nearly three months after entering Russian territory, Napoleon finally arrived in Moscow. But instead of finding supplies and sustenance for his malnourished and weather-beaten army, Napoleon discovered that nearly all the Russian food had been either taken or burned. After waiting a month for a Russian peace treaty that never came, Napoleon's army began to starve to death. Facing the onset of a brutal Russian winter, Napoleon and the French army retreated the same way they had come.

Within a matter of weeks, the French retreat had become a total route, and by the time Napoleon's Grande Armée crossed the Neman once more, they had lost more than four hundred thousand men. The once-applauded army had been decimated—not as a result of opposing military strength, but due to starvation and cold. Although a brilliant military tactician, Napoleon had neglected his men's most obvious need for food, and as a result, they withered, froze, and died.

The Enemy of Our Souls

The Russian general's keen strategy is similar to that of the Enemy of our souls. Satan employs attrition warfare. He seeks to deprive us of spiritual sustenance, because starved souls make for easy prey (1 Peter 5:8). He attacks us at our weakest moments. At times God's children give away the battle, not because they exhaust their spiritual resources, but because they don't use them at all. Believers are quick to forget we are in a battle, "not against flesh and blood, but against the rulers, against the powers, against the world forces of this darkness, against the spiritual forces of wickedness in the heavenly places" (Ephesians 6:12). The devil lurks; he prowls and is content that we would trust in Christ as Savior just as long as we do not trust Him to supply our every need (2 Corinthians 2:11). Satan cannot steal our salvation, but he can try to steal our peace and rob our joy (John 10:10). Our adversary is happy to find those whom he seeks to destroy failing to use the resources and wield the weapons God has provided in the heat of the battle.

Our Shield

In our battle against the devil and our own sinful flesh, God's Word is indeed our sword (Ephesians 6:17), but prayer is the shield by which we "extinguish all the flaming arrows of the evil one" (v. 16). To live prayerless is to live *defenseless* amid the battle. In Christ, God gives the Christian confidence, but He does not condone carelessness or negligence in regard to the strength and shielding our souls need the most. Jesus lived for forty days without food (Matthew 4:1–11), but He did not live for an hour without prayer (Luke 5:16). We need protection in battle, we need joy in the midst of sorrow, and we need communion with God in a confusing and chaotic world. We *need* prayer.

Jesus told His followers not to be anxious (Matthew 6:34), and more than any other command in Scripture we are told: "Do not fear" (Isaiah 41:10). But how is this possible? Our world is fractured, our lives are fleeting, and Satan is on the attack. How can I be "anxious for nothing" (Philippians 4:6 NKJV)? How can God wipe away my worries? How can I rejoice always (1 Thessalonians 5:16)?

Prayer.

And the stunning reality is that when you pray, *your Father hears*.

Pray about Everything

When Paul told the Philippians to "be anxious for nothing," he didn't stop there—he continued to say "but in everything by prayer and supplication, with thanksgiving, let your requests be made known to God" (Philippians 4:6 NKJV). And then what's the result? Paul said, "And the peace of God, which surpasses all understanding, will guard your hearts and minds through Christ Jesus" (v. 7 NKJV). Interestingly, Paul did not pen these words from his mahogany desk but from his Roman jail cell. Despite his grim circumstances, he wrote to rejoice always (Philippians 4:4), be anxious for nothing (Philippians 4:6), and pray about everything. This was Paul's prescription for worried and anxious minds: prayer.

Jesus told his anxious followers that our heavenly Father already knows all our needs (Matthew 6:8, 32), yet we are told to run to Him in prayer for everything in our lives. God doesn't want us to run to Him in prayer for only the "big things," but for *everything*. Why? Because "He cares about you" (1 Peter 5:7). He is not aloof or indifferent—He calls us to cast our burdens upon Him (Psalm 55:22). A Christian is indeed someone who has placed his or her faith in God (Romans 10:9), but biblical belief is not merely the *placement* of our faith in Christ; it's the continued *practice* and habit of faith as a constant exercise. Faith is not a *thing*; faith is an *action*. It has to do with where we set our minds and where we fix our gaze—and for the child of God, the exercise of faith is most practically expressed when we flee to our Father in prayer.

Fleeing to God as our refuge and relying on Him as our strength is merely Christian mumbo jumbo to those who are strangers to God in prayer. God *is* a "very present help in trouble" (Psalm 46:1), but His nearness and closeness are not equally sensed by everyone. Psalm 145:18 says that God is "near to all who call on Him." God's nearness is an *objective* fact, but it is also a *subjective* experience. His nearness is sensed in a real, comforting, and invigorating way only by those who "call on Him." When prayer is on the back burner of our lives, worry and anxiety will be on the forefront of our minds. If we are to divorce our lives from the worries of the world and defend ourselves against the flaming arrows of the adversary, we must run to our heavenly Father in prayer.

Previously we have examined both God's sovereignty and omniscience, and in light of these truths you may be tempted to think, *Why pray if God knows all my needs and is sovereign over them? If my Father knows all my needs before I ask Him [Matthew 6:8], why should I bring my needs before Him at all?* You are not alone in this type of thinking; therefore, in this chapter I want to address the *why* and *how* of prayer, knowing that the *when* of prayer is simple: "Pray without ceasing" (1 Thessalonians 5:17). Finally, I will address some common questions about prayer and provide the scriptural basis for why God hears our prayers in the first place. But before we continue, let me remind you that when you pray, *your Father hears.*

Why Pray?

Prayer Is a Command

Prayer is not a suggestion, nor is it an optional extra that Christians can discard; it is something Christians must do out of obedience. Jesus began His instruction on prayer by saying, "When you pray" (Matthew 6:5), not "If you pray," because the foregone assumption is that the children of God desire and delight to commune with their Father. Jesus told His disciples a parable "to show that at all times they ought to pray and not to lose heart" (Luke 18:1). Prayer is a duty; however, because God is a good Father, every command He gives us in Scripture is also for our good! In the same way I tell my daughter to eat her dinner because she will starve without it, God tells us to pray because without it our souls starve. In prayer, we exalt the glory of God, express our dependence on God, and plead for God's will to be done and for His kingdom to come. Prayer is not for *some* Christians. Nor is it just for grandmas, pastors, and super-saint soccer moms; it is for the everyday child of God. Prayer is a command. But it's more than that . . .

Prayer Is a Privilege

Prayer is far more than a duty. Prayer is the highest privilege we have as children of God. Stars cannot pray. Oceans cannot pray. The mountains cannot pray. The animals cannot pray. Why? Because they are not made in the image of God and redeemed by the blood of the Lamb (John 1:29). As a child of God, you *get* to pray because you are worth far more than all the stars, mountains, animals, and trees in the world combined. Sadly, this precious privilege is often neglected. People enter lotteries to meet celebrities, they pay hundreds, if not thousands, of dollars to get good seating at a concert or sporting event—I would even venture to say that many American men spend more time watching football on a single Sunday afternoon than they do in prayer the entire year combined. Why? Because we often become numb to the wonder of prayer. This isn't to say football is bad (go Bears), but it is to say that we have lost sight of the privilege prayer is and, in turn, have relegated prayer to the peripheral pockets of our lives. Prayer is fellowship and communion with our Creator, Savior, Friend, and the King of Kings. If someone were to write a biography on your life, would prayer be a main chapter? Would it even be included in the appendix?

Privileges are typically granted, not earned. And such is the case with prayer. Christ, by His obedience, death, and resurrection, has purchased this privilege for us. His Word tells us that when we go to God in prayer, He listens (1 John 5:14)! *Our heavenly Father hears.* To pray is not a natural birthright; it's a spiritual birthright in Christ. Jesus had to die so that you could approach God and call Him "Father." And this is surely the greatest weapon we possess as we face the anxieties and worries of life. It also must be understood that God does not want us to pray only when we are anxious; He wants us to "pray without ceasing." *Your Father wants a relationship with you*—a relationship that is a prerequisite to peace.

Prayer Is Powerful

Maybe you're still wondering, *Why pray if God is sovereign?* Well, first, because prayer is a duty; second, because prayer is a privilege; and, third, because prayer is indeed powerful! Not only does God ordain the end; *He also ordains the means to the end.* God does not need dirt to plant trees, or rain to nourish them, or the sun to help them grow, but he uses dirt, rain, and photosynthesis to accomplish His purpose. Similarly, God uses prayers to accomplish His will, and prayer does in fact change things!

- "Elijah was a human being, even as we are. He prayed earnestly that it would not rain, and it did not rain on the land for three and a half years" (James 5:17, NIV).
- Moses lacked fluidity of speech, he was afraid of Pharaoh, and yet he prayed and split the Red Sea and brought forth water from the rock (Exodus 17:4–6).
- Jonah had his many imperfections, yet he prayed and the fish spat him up on dry land (Jonah 2:10).
- Hezekiah was timid, and he prayed and the angel of the Lord wiped out 185,000 Assyrians (2 Kings 19:35).
- David prayed and God delivered him from all his fears (Psalm 34:4).
- Daniel prayed and God shut the lions' mouths (Daniel 6:22).
- The church prayed and an angel of the Lord delivered Peter from a Roman prison (Acts 12:1–17).

In the sixteenth century, Mary, Queen of Scots, said this of one Scottish minister: "I fear John Knox's prayer more than an army of ten thousand men."[1] Why? Because prayer is powerful.

A few years ago, while ministering with some friends in Kathmandu, Nepal, I watched Buddhist worshipers spin their prayer wheels over and over again. They believe that when a prayer is written and then attached to the wheel and spun, it multiplies their merit and prayers before Buddha. For Buddhists, spinning a prayer wheel is so powerful that it is likened to the power of one hundred monks praying their entire lives. But praying to Buddha availeth nothing. Why? Because Buddha is dead. He died 2,700 years ago. He cannot hear you. He does not and cannot answer your prayers. But our God is alive! He hears and answers our prayers. Prayer is powerful! Remember, our battle against anxiety and worry is waged in our minds. And, scripturally speaking, *your mind is the sum of your prayer life*. Have you ever considered the reality that your spiritual life is a direct reflection of your prayer life? Maybe you pray and yet still feel the onslaught of worry and fear. I ask you, Are you praying without ceasing? Our world, our flesh, and the devil never issue a ceasefire; therefore, God's Word tells us to "pray without ceasing" (1 Thessalonians 5:17). Corrie ten Boom said, "The Devil may laugh at our plans. He smiles when we are up to our eyes in work. But he quakes when we pray."[2] Why? Because prayer is powerful.

How Do We Pray?

Jesus did not instruct His anxious disciples on how to preach or cast out demons, but He did instruct them on how to pray (Luke 11:1–4). Large swords are the hardest to wield, and the powerful weapon of prayer is the hardest, but most necessary, thing for a Christian to learn and apply. God does grant peace and joy, but He does not offer compartmentalized victory in the Christian life. If we want to grow in one area of our Christian lives (for example, learning how to handle worry), we must pursue God holistically. We do not simply pray, "God take away my worry." We pray in this manner:

Lord, help me to love You; give me an exalted view of Your holiness and power. Thank You for all that You have done for me in Christ. Thank You for forgiving me of my sin. Thank You for preparing a home for me in heaven. Lord, today I pray that You would grant me the peace that comes from knowing that You are in total control of my life. I confess that my heart is prone to worry and despair, so, God, please forgive me of my worry and give me the joy only You can provide.

The vigor of our spiritual lives is the fruit of our prayer lives; therefore, understanding how to pray biblically is of utmost importance. Do you long to grow in this area of your relationship with God? I do. The ACTS (adoration, confession, thanksgiving, supplication) formula has long been used to provide a framework for how the believer should pray. And for the remainder of this chapter, my prayer is that you would glean the importance of each of these different principles in your prayer life and, as a result, have greater fellowship with your Savior, Jesus Christ. Remember, our battle against sinful worry and anxiety is won when we grow in our trust of our Father—and there can be no trust if there is no true communion in prayer.

Adoration

Immediately prior to His sermon on anxiety, Jesus taught His disciples how to pray (Matthew 6:9–14). My dad used to tell me, "Jonny, context is key," and such is the case when we come to Jesus' sermon on worry. In Matthew 6 we see a certain reality: a prayerless person will inevitably be an anxious person. And Jesus taught His followers to pray in a way that tunes our hearts to the goodness, power, and holiness of our Father. Jesus' manual on prayer begins not with our needs but with "our Father" (Matthew 6:9).

When we run to God as our refuge and strength, we flee not to an impersonal force or a detached shelter but to a loving and personal Father. Sadly, the perfunctory "Our Father" has become so normal in our prayers that we have become numb to the power and preciousness of it. Only fifteen times in the Old Testament is the term *father* used in a religious sense, but in the New Testament, *Father* is used 245 times. Why? Because of the work of Jesus Christ. "Father" is a term of endearment that drips with affection. Do you understand what this means? It means that the "rock" (Psalm 18:2) to which we run is "our Father" who wraps us in His arms. It would have seemed wildly presumptuous to the Jews to call God "Father," and yet this is the truth Jesus repeatedly engrained in His disciples. Following the resurrection, Jesus said, "Go to My brethren and say to them, 'I ascend to My Father and your Father'" (John 20:17). This is a stunning reality. About prayer, John Calvin wrote that we come to God in prayer the same way "children unburden their troubles to their parents."[3] Do you view prayer this way? This is unspeakably intimate, yet the One we call "Father" is also the One "which art in Heaven" (Matthew 6:9 KJV).

The reality of our Father's dwelling place reminds us once again that while we rush into God's presence *boldly* (Hebrews 4:16) through the blood of Jesus Christ, we do not enter His presence in prayer *flippantly*. Perhaps there is little comfort in our prayers because we often forget to whom we are praying. J. I. Packer said, "Drab thoughts of God make prayer dull."[4] At times, we may acknowledge that God is "our Father" but forget that He is "in heaven." In doing so, we lose sight of the fact that He is the sovereign King who upholds the universe (Hebrews 1:3), channels the hearts of kings (Proverbs 21:1), and holds our lives in His hands (Isaiah 41:13). According to Jesus' model, prayer begins with worship, not with *requests*. It begins by directing our gaze toward our Father "in heaven"—and then Jesus instructs us to pray in such a way as to hallow the name of God (Matthew 6:9–10). To clarify, this is not to say that we should not spontaneously make our requests known to God (Philippians 4:6), but that worshipful prayer tunes our hearts and transforms our perspectives, even if circumstances remain constant. To hallow God's name means that we remember that He is set apart and *holy*. It is to ascribe majesty unto the Lord (1 Chronicles 29:11). It is good to call on God "on the day of trouble" (Psalm 50:15), but our prayer lives should not be isolated to states of emergency. Praying to your Father only when you're in trouble would be like using your cell phone only when you need to dial 911.

Prayer reminds us *who we are* in light of *who our Father is*. But when the pattern of our prayer lives is exclusively requests, petitions, and wants, we lose one of the primary purposes of prayer, which is to hallow the name of God. Our prayer lives will inevitably be anemic when we come to God only with a grocery list of "gets." But when our hearts' desire is foremost the hallowing of His name and the advancement of His kingdom (Matthew 6:10), all our other needs and desires are put into perspective (v. 33).

Are you as anxious about the glory of God as you are about your personal desires? When was the last time you prayed this kind of prayer:

> God, bring the light of Your truth into this dark world! Father, Your kingdom come and Your will be done—and, Lord, start with me! Make me do Your will! The world is full of people who do not obey Your Word or do Your will, but, O God, unite my heart to fear Your name [Psalm 86:11]!

Adoration tunes our hearts to God's glory, power, and authority, and if we miss this crucial element of prayer, our petitions will lack perspective of who we are praying to, and, consequently, our worries will not be wiped away no matter how hard we plead.

Confession

I remember enduring the heat waves that came through Southern California when I was a boy. The once-green hillsides, trees, and lawns would turn to a pale brown; what once looked vibrant now lacked vitality under the pounding heat of the sun. David said this is what unconfessed sin does to our souls. It drains away our vitality "as with the fever heat of summer" (Psalm 32:4). Harbored sin is like a vacuum that sucks the joy and vibrancy out of our Christian life—it is as though a thick fog blurs our fellowship with God. Therefore, the Bible calls us to confess our sin so that we might find mercy (Proverbs 28:13). As Christians, we do not fear condemnation, for "there is now no condemnation at all for those who are in Christ Jesus" (Romans 8:1). We have already been justified through faith and are "at peace with God" (Romans 5:1). Sin in the life of a believer does not steal our salvation, but it can steal our joy (Psalm 51:12). Therefore sin does not nullify our adoption as children of God, but it does fracture our fellowship with our Father and grieve the Holy Spirit (Ephesians 4:30).

When we sin, our security in Christ cannot be removed, but our confidence in our security—our assurance—can be affected. When we lose assurance of our peace *with* God, we will inevitably forfeit the peace *of* God that comes to His children. This doesn't mean that when we sin, we are *less* Christian, but it's only to say that when our fellowship with our Father is fractured because of sin, it is very possible that our confidence in our adoption will be as well. Among several other names, Satan is known as *the accuser* (Revelation 12:10; Romans 8:33). Why? Because he seeks to bring our sins before the Father and remind Him of how wretched and sinful His children really are. Satan cannot steal our salvation, but he can sow doubt in our minds about whether we truly belong to God. He whispers, *Look at your sin,* when God preaches to us in His Word, *Look to Jesus* (Hebrews 12:2).

To confess our sins is to admit our sins transparently and humbly before God and to agree with His diagnosis of our hearts' condition. We ask for forgiveness and confess specifically and honestly our sin, not to be justified once again, but because we want the joy and peace of a clean conscience and for our fellowship and communion with our Father to be restored. Indeed, a pricked conscience is the underlying cause of much anxiety. The conscience is God's gift to His beloved children—it warns us when our souls are in danger and when we have sin to confess.

What's the promise to those who confess their sins?

"If we confess our sins, He is faithful and righteous to forgive us our sins and to cleanse us from all unrighteousness" (1 John 1:9). Our gracious God has promised that those who come to Him will have their sins removed "as far as the east is from the west" (Psalm 103:12). Moreover, God purifies us not only from our sin; He also purifies and softens our polluted and hardened consciences (Hebrews 9:14). Have you ever wondered, *What's the result of the believer's confession of sin?* You may say "forgiveness," which would be true, but it's more than that. Psalm 130:4 says, "There is forgiveness with You, that You may be feared." God's forgiveness leads to fear—not in the sense of dread, but in the sense of humble awe and wonder. Confession is a catalyst to awe, and awe is the on-ramp to worship.

Thanksgiving

Prayer and praise are twins. Paul wrote, *"Be anxious for nothing, but in everything by prayer and supplication, with thanksgiving, let your requests be made known to God"* (Philippians 4:6 NKJV, emphasis added). Have you ever thought about how thanksgiving is a scriptural remedy for anxiety? The Bible teaches that thanksgiving serves as both the foundation and walls of our prayer. We come to God and thank Him, not only when He answers our prayers, but for listening to our prayers at all. We thank Him not only for what He does but for *who He is.*

One of the reasons we are prone to worry is that we are often so ungrateful. And because our lives are short on praise, they are short on peace. In a previous chapter, we examined the art of meditation and how we are to "chew" on the character and promises of God, and one of the ways we do that is by expressing thanks to our Father in prayer. If we do not come *thankfully* into God's presence, we will come *greedily.* A. W. Tozer said, "Prayer among evangelical Christians is always in danger of degenerating into a glorified gold rush."[5] Without thanksgiving, we come to God as though He were a vending machine. In Luke 17, Jesus healed ten lepers, but only one came back to say thank you. We can look down on the nine lepers who didn't thank Jesus, but are we so different? Do we come to God gratefully thanking Him for cleansing each day? Not from leprous skin, but from our leprous hearts.

Interestingly, Paul's prescription for anxious minds includes thanksgiving, and if it is part of the prescription, it is often a component of the diagnosis—*thankless hearts produce anxious minds.* Do you come before God and thank Him for all He has done? For who He is? Do you thank Him for His sovereignty amid troubling times? Do you thank Him that He hears your prayers (Psalm 4:3)? Do you thank Him for the work of Christ on your behalf?

Supplication

Prayer is an expression of our dependence on God. Jesus instructed His disciples to pray, "Give us this day our daily bread" (Matthew 6:11), and Paul said, "By prayer and supplication . . . let your requests be made known to God" (Philippians 4:6). We pray that God would grant us our "daily bread" because each day we need to be reminded that we are not strong or sufficient enough to survive on our own. God gave the Israelites manna one day at a time so that they would learn the habit of coming to God with their needs each and every day. Far too often, we live as if we personally provide for ourselves and then call on God only when we are "in a pickle" (as my dad used to say). In Jesus' model, however, we ask our Father to meet our daily needs, trusting Him to do so, and then thanking Him when He does.

Praying that God would grant us our needs is not a mindless ritual but rather a confession that the economy can tank, our careers are not impenetrable, ACLs can tear, scholarships can be removed, and global peace can dissipate. Our lives are much more fragile than we think. Therefore, each day is a renewed declaration of our dependence on God. When we worry about tomorrow, we are living in tomorrow today, but God gives us strength and grace for only one day at a time. The apostle Peter wrote, "Therefore humble yourselves under the mighty hand of God, that He may exalt you at the proper time, casting all your anxiety on Him, because He cares for you" (1 Peter 5:6–7). When believers make their requests known to God, they do so not to an annoyed deity but to a loving and caring Father. As our Father, God cares about our needs far more than we do. To doubt this is to doubt the very character of God. Doubt is the opposite of dependence—it is defiance. It is a defamation of the character of our God. When we worry, we are saying, *Father, You are not sovereign. Father, You are not wise. Father, You are not loving. Father, You do not care for me.*

We make supplication to God because we live in a world of trouble and pain. And the peace of God does not come from denying trouble but by bringing our trouble to God. When we pray, we do not need to twist God's arm to get Him to listen (as if we could), but rather, as Calvin said, we climb into our Father's lap and whisper our needs into His ear.

When God Says No

Maybe you have heard someone say, "God always answers prayers." But this is not *always* true. Let me give you a few examples:

1. In Scripture there are instances when God's people persisted in pursuing their sin and then called on God in prayer only to fix their problems. This is a type of prayer that God *doesn't* hear. "They have turned their backs to Me, and not their faces; but in the time of their trouble they will say, 'Arise and save us!'" (Jeremiah 2:27). The psalmist said, "If I regard wickedness in my heart, the Lord will not hear" (Psalm 66:18). George Müller said, "It is not possible to live in sin, and at the same time, by communion with God, draw down from heaven everything one needs for this life."[6]

2. We can pray with wrong motives (James 4:3), and as a result God will not answer our prayers. God answers prayers that are in accordance with His will and His kingdom, not our will and our kingdom. This isn't to say that God is not the giver of good gifts! He is! But we shouldn't be surprised when God doesn't answer our prayers that are more in alignment with our desires than with His.

3. God's children are often their own answers to prayer. In other words, we pray often for revival, but we seldom proclaim Christ. We pray for a job, but we don't diligently apply and interview. We pray for an unsaved friend or relative and yet we have not been persistent in pleading with them in the truth. We, as God's children, are dependent on our Father, but dependence does not disqualify our diligence in obedience.

4. It must also be noted that sometimes God delays His answers to our prayers. But be encouraged: God's delays aren't

necessarily His denials. Paul prayed three times for his thorn to be removed, yet each time he was told no so that he would learn to fall on God's strength. If God had answered Paul's prayer the first time, he never would have learned to say, *God's grace is sufficient for me, and His power is made perfect in my weakness. Therefore, I will boast all the more in my weakness, so that the power of Christ may dwell in me* (2 Corinthians 12:9).

5. Sometimes God does not grant our requests because they are not in alignment with His perfect will for His glory and our eternal good. For example, Margaret Clarkson prayed her entire life for a husband and never received one. She found peace and comfort in the truth of God's sovereignty and care, saying, "Why must I live my life alone? I do not know. But Jesus Christ is Lord of my life. I believe in the sovereignty of God, and I accept my singleness from his hand. He could have ordered my life otherwise, but he has not chosen to do so. As his child, I must trust his love and wisdom."[7] Sometimes God does say no. But His denials are always for our best.

6. As we talk about unanswered prayers, we must also realize that unanswered prayers are not always our biggest problem. What is, then? James 4:2 says, "You do not have because you do not ask." Therefore, the biggest problem in our lives is not unanswered prayers but *unoffered* prayers to God. Consider the words of the beloved hymn "What a Friend We Have in Jesus":

> What a Friend we have in Jesus, all our sins and
>   griefs to bear!
> What a privilege to carry everything to God in
>   prayer!
> O what peace we often forfeit, O what needless pain
>   we bear,

all because we do not carry everything to God in
prayer.
Have we trials and temptations? Is there trouble
anywhere?
We should never be discouraged; take it to the Lord
in prayer.
Can we find a friend so faithful who will all our
sorrows share?
Jesus knows our every weakness; take it to the Lord
in prayer.

Often, those who say that God has not answered their prayers are those who do not carry everything to God in prayer in the first place.

These are some of the reasons God may or may not be answering your prayers. But the testimony of Scripture is that when we pray, God hears and He answers. Isaiah 65:24 says, "Before they call, I will answer; and while they are still speaking, I will hear." God hears our prayers, and often when we pray according to the will of God, we get what we truly need, even if it's not what we asked for. If our hearts' desire is to see our Father glorified and His kingdom advanced and His will be done, then everything else can be entrusted to Him as well (Matthew 6:33). When we come to God with a heart for His honor, prayer extends to us what we really need—even if we don't receive what we asked for.

What Is the Fruit of Prayer?

As a good Father, God instructs His children to pray for their own benefit! Prayer fosters holiness, communion, and blessing in our lives. David said, "How blessed is the man who takes refuge in Him!" (Psalm 34:8). When we run to God in prayer, we can say with the sons of Korah, "Therefore we will not fear" (Psalm 46:2). We live in a dark and hostile world and yet the Christian is told to be courageous and strong (Ephesians 6:10). How is this possible? Through prayer—a courageous spine is dependent on bruised knees. You will never stand tall in biblical courage unless you kneel in pleading prayer. If we are to smash to smithereens our worries and fears, then we must hold up the shield of faith that blocks the blows of Beelzebub. H. B. Charles said, "The Christian life is a battle-ground, not a playground"[8]; therefore, if you want to be on the front lines and not hiding in the barracks, bow down to God in prayer and He will give you strength. Trust in God is the product of communion *with* God. Where there is no fellowship, there will never be any deep faith. You cannot get to know anyone in an intimate and personal way if you talk to them for only a couple of moments each day. Again, *when prayer is on the back burner of our lives, anxiety will be on the forefront of our minds.*

What Gives Us Confidence in Prayer?

Why does God hear our prayers? Because we come to Him "in Christ." Hebrews 7:25 says that Jesus "always lives to make intercession" for us. Have you considered this stunning thought? Christian, right now Jesus is interceding and praying for you to the Father. He still prays for His sheep just as He did when He was on earth. We don't know how to pray, we mumble and bumble, we lisp and stammer, at times we pretend and posture, but thankfully Jesus intercedes for us and so does His Holy Spirit—who intercedes for us "with groanings too deep for words" (Romans 8:26). Our poor and pitiful prayers are powerful because of the blood of our High

Priest, Jesus Christ, and the work of His Spirit. J. C. Ryle said: "The bank-note without a signature at the bottom is nothing but a worthless piece of paper. The stroke of a pen confers on it all its value."[9] We can bring nothing to the Father outside of Christ's necessary signature, which He has written with His own precious blood.

A Man Who Prayed

I remember reading the biography of George Müller when I was a boy. This Englishman ministered in churches and orphanages during the nineteenth century at a time when orphans lived in Oliver Twistesque conditions. During Müller's ministry, he cared for more than two thousand orphans at a time, and even though his needs were many, he never mentioned them to anyone other than his heavenly Father in prayer. In his journal, Müller recorded more than fifty thousand specific recorded answers to prayer—that's more than five hundred answers to prayer every year! Müller's life not only serves as an example of a man who prayed fervently but, more importantly, functions as the validation of what we have been examining: *your Father hears your prayers.*

Müller went on to detail that God proves Himself to be the "living God" to those who pursue Him in prayer. Our trust in God will only be as deep as our prayer lives. Each day is a renewed battle against the arrows of the adversary; therefore, Müller said, "I saw more clearly than ever, that the first great and primary business to which I ought to attend every day was, to have my soul happy in the Lord."[10]

Do you pray? Do you plead with God on your knees? The world in which we live is fraught with fear, and perhaps your own heart may be filled with fear and worry as well. Could it be that part of your problem is that you do not run to God in prayer? Could it be that you come to Him only with supplication and rarely with the adoration He deserves? Is there something you need to confess to God? Oh, Christian, pray often! Why? Because, as John Bunyan said, "prayer is a shield to the soul, a sacrifice to God, and a scourge for Satan."[11]

—— Reflection Questions ——

1. Read Philippians 4:6 again. How does thankful prayer relate to worry and anxiety?

2. What are some examples in Scripture that showcase the power and efficacy of prayer? What stories in your life testify to the power of prayer?

3. Why is confession essential to our relationship with God? How does the knowledge of God's forgiveness help us in regard to anxiety and worry (1 John 1:9)?

PART III

Our Way Forward

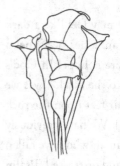

CHAPTER 13

Mission,
Family, Future

I'm a preacher, and I'm also the son of a preacher, and one of the first things they teach about *preaching* is that the end of a sermon is not a crash landing in which you simply remark, "Oh, well, folks, apparently I'm out of time. I guess you're all dismissed." But rather, in every good sermon, there is a clear conclusion—a point, principle, summation, implication, or application that encapsulates the message and helps the body of Christ think through the question "What now?"

Have you ever wondered, *How did Jesus conclude His sermon on anxiety?* He called His anxious followers to contemplate their heavenly Father's character—but not only that—He then commissioned them to engage in their heavenly Father's kingdom work. He gave them marching orders. Jesus said, "Do not worry," then added, "Seek first His kingdom and His righteousness, and all these things will be added to you" (Matthew 6:31, 33). You are likely familiar with this verse but may have overlooked its immediate context. Jesus told

His followers that the antidote to anxiety is not only truth we contemplate with our minds but a life of service that involves our hands and feet. God sets our feet upon the rock—not in wet cement. He wants us to move. Right thinking is valuable only if it leads to right action. Therefore, God not only casts out our fear, but He calls us into His kingdom's service.

To the anxious and despairing, life itself may feel like a dark and muddy pit. Our fears surround us, our anxieties overwhelm us, and our despair weighs us down. But there is hope! In God's kindness He rescues us. He reaches down into the black abyss we find ourselves in, grabs hold of us, and sets our feet upon the rock and gives us a firm place to stand (Psalm 40:2). We have previously examined God's kindness and power to sustain all who have fallen (Psalm 145:14), revive those who are troubled and distressed (Psalm 71:20), and lift up the heads of the weary (Psalm 3:3). We must go one step further, however: God not only gives us ground to stand on, but He also provides the pathway forward.

As we engage in service to God, His people, and His kingdom, God is going to do three things in our hearts: First, He is going to lift our gaze from the chaos and unrighteousness of this world and onto His righteous plans and purposes. Second, in serving God, we are reminded that we are not an only child in His family but "fellow citizens with God's people and also members of his household" (Ephesians 2:19 NIV). Every Christian does have a personal relationship with Jesus, but not a private one. No one is a lone ranger in our Father's family. And third, as we consider our Father's kingdom, we are reminded that "the world is passing away" (1 John 2:17), but our Father's kingdom is eternal (2 Peter 1:11). This world is not our home—heaven is—and one day we will meet our Savior face-to-face and be free, once and for all, from the worries and the anxieties of this world.

In this chapter I want to examine these three critical truths, without which our understanding and course of action in our pursuit of God's peace will be deficient and, consequently, of no lasting value.

Your Father's Kingdom

Mount Carmel was the high point of Elijah's prophetic ministry; there he called down fire from heaven, declared Yahweh to be the only true God, and defeated the false prophets of Baal. If Carmel was the pinnacle of Elijah's career (literally and metaphorically), then the scene that followed in Jezreel (1 Kings 19) must have been rock bottom. As we examined in a previous chapter, after his duel with the prophets of Baal, Elijah had great hopes of a national spiritual reform. But Elijah's expectations of a national revival were shattered as he returned to Jezreel and found out that Jezebel was seeking to kill him. In response, "Elijah was afraid and ran for his life" (1 Kings 19:3 NIV). The prophet then went a day's journey into the wilderness, brooded over his ministerial failure, fell into a black pit of despair, and prayed, "It is enough; now, O Lord, take my life, for I am not better than my fathers" (1 Kings 19:4). We have already considered God's kindness in coming to Elijah and nourishing his soul and body, but we have not yet examined what God said next: "Go, return on your way to the wilderness of Damascus" (1 Kings 19:15). It's easy to gloss over verses such as these, but this is significant. The One who had come to Elijah to *refresh* and *replenish* him physically and spiritually was now going to *recommission* him for His kingdom work. God reclaimed Elijah from his wanderings, soothed and strengthened him, set him back on his feet, and said in a graceful yet direct tone: *Get back to work.*

Remember, our Father is mindful of our form (Psalm 103:14). He knows our genetic constitution. He created our temperamental makeup. And He knows (better than anyone) that a solitary environment, with no clear course of action, is not the remedy to our anxious fears and despondency; rather, it is one of the causes. This is not to say that silence and solitude are foreign to the Christian life, for "Jesus Himself would often slip away to the wilderness and pray" (Luke 5:16), but prolonged silence and solitude devoid of Christ's mission aggravate rather than ameliorate our despair. In God's grace, God gives us work to do. Elijah may have been plunged into further depths of despair and greater degrees of despondency and anxiety if not for the employing call of God on his life. God is gracious in both His comfort and in His commissions. Repeatedly throughout Scripture, God's medicine to the despairing and anxious is an assignment that He gave to them for the advancement of His kingdom and the benefit of others. After Peter's triple denial of Jesus, God was gracious, not only in His forgiveness, but in His renewed commission to Peter. Peter was all but ready to leave the ministry; he said, "I am going fishing" (John 21:3). But Jesus came to Peter, recommissioned him, and said, "Feed my sheep" (v. 16 KJV). Similarly, in the midst of Jesus' magnum opus on anxiety, He did not merely say "Do not be anxious"; He commissioned His followers to engage in His heavenly work. Why did Jesus do this? Because He knows that as we participate in what He is doing, the attention of our hearts is transferred from the broken, painful, and fleeting realities of this world to His righteous and eternal kingdom. In seeking God's kingdom, we become more and more aware of His power and provision, and therefore our trust that "all these things will be added to you" (Matthew 6:33) grows exponentially within our hearts.

Maybe you're wondering, *What does seeking first God's kingdom and His righteousness look like practically?* In a *positional* sense, it means we come to God in saving faith; in a *progressive* sense, it means we seek Christlikeness; but in a *purposeful* sense, it means we have no greater joy than to *serve* the citizens of Christ's kingdom and *reach* those who remain outside it. Heavenly pursuits and earthly anxieties are not mutually exclusive, but Jesus does say that the former will drive out the latter. God's faithful servants war against worry and walk through sloughs of despondency, but the antidote to our anxiety and the remedy for our melancholy is never to retire from the ministry but to press on in doing what God has put before us. Throughout this book I have reiterated the reality that the child of God is to give thanks always (1 Thessalonians 5:18), but God's thankful children provide tangible evidence of their gratitude by serving others in God's family. Ministering to other people, bearing one another's burdens, and employing our spiritual gifts may feel like a separate subject for a separate book, but in the Great Physician's treatment plan, service in His kingdom is corrective, healing, and liberating. Joy and service are in a symbiotic relationship. Joy fuels service and service accelerates and invigorates greater degrees of joy. The most joyful people on earth are those who do not live for themselves. Service is the gift that keeps giving. Some people wonder why they are so forlorn, and often (not always) it is because they have not sought someone to serve. Are you anxious? Are you despairing? Is it possible that you are waiting for someone else to serve you instead of thinking creatively and strategically about whom you can serve? Are you waiting for someone to meet your needs instead of considering how you can meet the needs of others? Perhaps you are familiar with the story of Joni Eareckson Tada—she has been paralyzed from the neck down since the age of seventeen—yet her heart to serve others is remarkable. I'll never forget reading an article she wrote titled "How Quadriplegia Prepared Me to Carry Others."[1] Joni reflected on the reality that her greatest trial is also her greatest opportunity to serve, comfort, and minister to other people. And, in doing so, her life, albeit difficult, is full of joy. Whenever she is downcast, Joni said she "sings her way through suffering" and determines to "serve others who hurt worse than I do."[2] What a remarkable testimony. Do you see the trials in your life this way?

In the midst of our anxiety and despair, there is the temptation to stop, collapse, and throw in the towel—to give up. Our worries seem to keep piling up and so do the bills to pay, laundry to fold, and meals to prepare. Elisabeth Elliot was faced with similar temptations as she endured the deaths of, not one, but two husbands. Her first husband, Jim, died when she was only thirty years old. With a ten-month-old daughter in her arms, Elisabeth was confronted with the question *Do I really trust God?* Thirteen years after Jim died, Elisabeth remarried. But after the third year of her new marriage, her second husband was diagnosed with cancer—he died less than a year later. Although confused and bewildered at the tremendous amount of pain and loss she had endured, Elisabeth's response to her trials is an inspiration to us all: trust in the Lord, obey His Word, and do the next thing. It would have been easy for Elisabeth Elliot to slip into the sinking sand of self-pity and despair, but her response to pain and sorrow was always to "do the next thing."[3] In our pain and sorrow, we do not always know what to do, so we do nothing. Our worries are like sharks circling around the prey of our minds. Fear begins to strangle our hope. Worry suffocates all our joy. And as a result the anxious, despairing, and fearful may lack the motivation to even get out of bed. They ask themselves, *What's the point?* But Elisabeth inspires us to take our eyes off the mound of worries and instead to fix our eyes on Christ and "do the next thing." Whatever that may be—bills, groceries, applications, interviews, hospital exams, and so on. God has not called us to live in the future, He has called us to live and serve in the present. God rescues us from the pit of self-pity, as He did for Elijah and Peter, as we rest in His character, move forward in trust, and do the next thing.

> Strong in His faithfulness, praise and sing.
> Then, as He beckons thee, do the next thing.[4]

Your Father's Family

You cannot live the Christian life alone. In our hyperindividualistic culture, we read a book on God's character as the remedy to our anxiety and then believe we can implement these truths *by ourselves*. But remember, there are no solo citizens in God's kingdom—no one is an only child in the family of God. Believers do experience a *personal* relationship with Jesus Christ, but our relationship with God is not merely personal; it is also corporate. Christians are sheep with one common Shepherd, children with one common Father, and citizens with one common King.

This is not a book on the church, but it is a book about trusting God in an anxious world—and the truth is that faith flourishes in the context of community. Our sorrows, troubles, and trials are heaviest when we bear them alone. Ironically, in our contemporary context, "friendships" abound on social platforms and yet very few people experience the deep, meaningful, sharpening, and uplifting relationships that the Bible describes. It's no coincidence that Elijah's despair came on the heels of a three-and-a-half-year period of loneliness. It's no coincidence that David's anxiety and fear was typically tethered to his isolation as he fled from his father-in-law Saul. It's also no coincidence that Paul wrote "Be anxious for nothing" when he was chained to his Roman guard, stripped of the fellowship and community that he had grown to love. In our individualistic world, believers often forget that we cannot live the Christian life alone, neither can we face the problems of today or the anxieties of tomorrow without our siblings in Christ to pick us up.

As believers, not only do we belong to God, but we also belong to one another in the local church (Romans 12:5). Why does the entire body hurt when one part is injured? Because each part of the body composes the indivisible whole. Along that same line, individual members of the body cannot and do not grow when they are disconnected from other members of the body. Our spiritual growth—learning to trust God more and remove ungodly worry from our lives—is a result of our sense of dependence on God and on His people. King Solomon said, "Two are better than one . . . for if either of them falls, the one will lift up his companion. But woe to the one who falls when there is not another to lift him up!" (Ecclesiastes 4:9–10). Fellow believers are not just friends, they are partners in the Christian life.

Believers are to do the following:

1. Devote themselves to one another (Acts 2:42). Is this the habit of your life?

2. Confess their sins to one another (James 5:16). Believers are given the gift of transparent confession, not only before God, but before other believers who might point us to God's grace, forgiveness, and restoration. Is there a joy-sucking sin in your life that needs to be confessed? To God and to others?

3. Forgive one another (Colossians 3:13). In the same way God forgives us, we need to forgive one another. Bitterness calcifies the soul and robs it of peace, but forgiveness brings much joy.

4. Serve one another (Galatians 5:13). Many people walk into the church today with the mindset of "Who is going to serve me?" instead of asking "Whom can I serve?" It's hard to be self-centered and full of self-pity when we are selflessly considering and meeting the needs of others (1 Peter 4:10).

5. Pray for one another (James 5:16). I have already highlighted the vital importance of prayer in the believer's life. What's interesting, however, is that Jesus' model prayer possesses zero first-person singular pronouns. Jesus didn't teach us to pray "*My* Father, who is in heaven . . . give *me my* daily bread." He taught us to pray, "*Our* Father . . . give *us* . . . forgive *us* . . .

lead *us* . . . deliver *us* . . ." (Matthew 6:9–13, emphasis added). Jesus presupposed that His Father's children pray *together*. We don't need to battle our anxiety and despair alone; we are to do so alongside other members in the body of Christ. Worry loses power when believers battle in prayer together.

6. Stimulate one another to love and good deeds (Hebrews 10:24). Sometimes believers need to be comforted, and at other times they need to be spurred on. When our trust in God wanes, when our confidence in His sovereignty dissipates, and when our zeal to serve Him dwindles, our siblings in Christ come alongside us and propel us to "press on" (Philippians 3:14).

7. Bear one another's burdens (Galatians 6:2). Are you carrying a heavy burden? Don't carry it alone. Our God comforts us in our affliction "so that we will be able to comfort those who are in any affliction with the comfort with which we ourselves are comforted by God" (2 Corinthians 1:4).

8. Love one another (John 13:34). First Peter 1:22 says, "Love one another with a pure heart fervently" (KJV). That word for "fervently," *ektenos*, means to love someone to the max. Love is the glue that bonds the children of God together. Christians share in their love for one another because they share a common love for Jesus Christ. We cannot live the Christian life without other Christians who love us and care for us. Indeed, one of the ways God loves His children is by giving us siblings in Christ so we might manifest His love to one another.

9. Build up one another (1 Thessalonians 5:11; Romans 14:19). In Acts 4 we are introduced to a man named Joseph, a Levite from Cyprus. You may be unfamiliar with that name because he is most commonly known by his nickname: Barnabas—which means "son of encouragement." Barnabas

had a reputation for encouraging and edifying the saints. In a world of discouragement, pain, anxiety, and affliction, be a Barnabas—be someone who strengthens and builds the souls of others.

10. Teach one another (Colossians 3:16). Believers are to feed on the Word of God personally, in study and meditation; corporately, as we sit under the teaching of Scripture in the church; and relationally, as we teach and sing the truth to one another throughout the week. Teaching the truth to someone who is anxious or despairing doesn't mean we say, "It's all going to be okay." Instead, it means we say, "Can I remind you of what you may already know? Can I tell you what God is teaching me in His Word that has provided me with peace?" There are times when God's people need to just *sit* with the downcast and despairing and not feel the urge to *teach*. But Christians are called to mutually employ the Word of God to strengthen each other's faith. In doing so, we realize something crucial: fixing our gaze and feeding our faith is a community project.

When we are disconnected from other Christians in the church, we not only rob others, but we also rob ourselves. When we are worried, other believers come alongside us to meet our needs and point us to the truth of our heavenly Father. When we are fearful, they remind us of God's sovereignty and supply us with the courage we lack. When we are depressed, they may just weep with us or sit with us and say nothing, or they may remind us of the joy we have in Christ. Our relationships within our Father's family are to be so deeply formed that we mourn with those who mourn, rejoice with those who rejoice, and suffer with those who suffer (1 Corinthians 12). Jesus' final prayer in the garden stressed His desire for His followers to be one in essence, one in shared life, one in will, and one in mutual love for one another. Much has been said about the character of our heavenly Father in this book, but *orthodoxy produces orthopraxy*. In other words, the truths of God's Word lead not only to right thoughts, but right actions amongst His children.

Your Father's Home

Hours before His crucifixion, Jesus told His disciples, "Do not let your heart be troubled; believe in God, believe also in Me" (John 14:1). In the shadow of the cross, the One who should have been *comforted* is instead *the comforter* (2 Corinthians 1:3). The disciples had followed Jesus, they had served Jesus, they had loved Jesus, and now Jesus had told them He was going to be taken away and killed. Their hearts were heavy with anxiety and despair; their future was unknown. Jesus had previously told the disciples plainly, "The Son of Man is to be delivered into the hands of men, and they will kill Him" (Mark 9:31), and now the hour of His agony had come. Jesus would soon be betrayed, tried, scourged, mocked, and crucified. And yet, in the moments leading up to His betrayal, Jesus would speak immensely comforting and precious words to His distraught disciples. He did not give them a pie-in-the-sky futuristic outlook—in fact, He promised them, "In this world you will have trouble" (John 16:33 NIV). Jesus, knowing that the minds and hearts of His disciples were flooded with uncertainties regarding the present and anxieties regarding the future, grounded their thinking in something, some *place*, that is sure—*heaven*.

Immediately after telling His disciples "Do not let your heart be troubled . . ." (John 14:1), Jesus said to them, "In My Father's house are many dwelling places; if it were not so, I would have told you; for I go to prepare a place for you. If I go and prepare a place for you, I will come again and receive you to Myself, that where I am, there you may be also" (vv. 2–3). The question that haunts mankind is the one that Job asked: "If a man dies, will he live again?" (Job 14:14).

What happens when we die?

Does life go beyond the grave? Is the idea of "eternal life" just a figment of a faulty imagination?

To such questions, Jesus answered, "I am going to prepare a place for you."

People prepare great things for those whom they love. This week my oldest daughter turned two years old, and this afternoon we will celebrate her birthday with friends and loved ones (bounce houses, bubbles, doughnuts, and so forth—you get the picture). Not everyone is a party planner, but everyone who loves someone else dearly understands that preparing great things for the people you love is not a chore, it is a delight. If we understand this on a human level (tainted by sin), how much more will our loving, kind, and compassionate Savior prepare wonderful things for those whom He has bought with His own blood?

Christian, do you doubt that Jesus is preparing a place for you?

Jesus said, "If it were not so, I would have told you." Jesus was saying, in effect, "If the hope of heaven were a myth of human hope, I would have told you plainly. I have never lied, never exaggerated, never dramatized reality. I have never shortened or stretched the truth." Karl Marx once claimed that religion is the opiate of the masses, but our Savior, for whom lying is "impossible" (Hebrews 6:18), promises palatial accommodations for His own in His Father's house. Are you worried about something in the near or distant future? Jesus says that your eternal future is with Him in glory. Heaven is not an overbooked motel but the dwelling place of God, and when you pass through death's door, you are immediately ushered into the presence of your Savior (2 Corinthians 5:8). Jesus said that He will take us to Himself, so that where He is, there we will be also. This is the first, simplest, and best part of heaven: Jesus is there. J. C. Ryle said, "I am a dying man in a dying world; all before me is unseen: the world to come is a harbour unknown! But Christ is there, and that is enough."[5] Remember, our spiritual lives are a product of our thought lives. Jesus tells the anxious to think! And one of the greatest truths worried and despairing believers can meditate on is our future home with Christ. Colossians 3:1–4 says, "Therefore if you have been raised with Christ, keep seeking the things that are above, where Christ is, seated at the right hand of God. *Set your minds on the things that are above,* not on the things that are on earth. For you have died, and your life is hidden with Christ in God. When Christ, who is our life, is revealed, then you also will be revealed with Him in glory" (emphasis added). Is this the habit of your life? To set your mind on things above? As you read these words, maybe you're asking, *What is heaven like? What are the "things" above that I am to set my mind on?*

What Is Heaven Like?

It's somewhat sad, but most Christians have heard very few sermons on the place where they will spend eternity. But don't you long to know what heaven will be like? In 1 Corinthians 2:9, Paul said, "Things which eye has not seen and ear has not heard, and which have not entered the human heart, all that God has prepared for those who love Him." People often use these words to detail that our future home in glory is wonderfully unimaginable (which is true), but we must always remember to read the next verse as well: "For to us God revealed them through the Spirit; for the Spirit searches all things, even the depths of God" (v. 10). Christians do have something unimaginable to look forward to, but the point that Paul was making here is that God has already revealed to us (in part) what He is preparing for those in Christ. God has not left us in the dark; He tells us what He is preparing "through the Spirit" (2 Corinthians 2:10).

So, what is heaven like?

The Bible generally describes heaven by detailing what it's not like in order to demonstrate what it will be like. For example, against the backdrop of our perishing, defiled, and fleeting world, the Bible says that our Father's house is a place that is imperishable, undefiled, and unfading (1 Peter 1:4). In heaven, our Savior will "wipe away every tear" from our eyes (Revelation 21:4). Because our Father is holy, His house will not be tainted by sin or the effects of sin. This means that in heaven there will be no gossip, lust, anger, malice, or greed. Furthermore, it will be a home without even the remotest *temptation* to sin. At the conclusion of time, our God will make "all things new" (v. 5), and in doing so He will eradicate every effect of man's fall (Genesis 3)—this includes worry, anxiety, and despair. At times we imagine that in heaven we are merely disembodied spirits, floating like wispy clouds in the sky, but God's Word teaches us that our eternal home is the new earth (Revelation 21:1). We will not be floating spirits but resurrected bodies in a physical place that God *remakes.* There will be no cancer, blindness, deafness, heartache, sorrow, or pain. Don't you long for that day? But heaven is not only the absence of corruption and chaos; it is the presence of all that a believer should long for:

1. Our Father is there. Jesus said, "Let your light shine before men in such a way that they may see your good works, and glorify your Father [pay attention here] who is *in heaven*" (Matthew 5:16, emphasis added). The reason heaven is your future home is because you have been adopted into the Father's family. Our Father's character buoys our anxious and despairing hearts in the weary world in which we live, but our Father's home is the anchor of our souls.

2. Not only is our Father in heaven, but so is our Savior, Jesus Christ. In the moments before His crucifixion, Jesus prayed, "Father, I desire that they also, whom You have given Me, be with Me where I am" (John 17:24). The reason you will be with Christ for all eternity is because Jesus desires that you *be with Him where He is.* In heaven you will dwell with the One who died for your sins, knows your name, and loves you perfectly. Don't you long for that day?

3. Our inheritance is in heaven. Did you know that you are a joint heir with Christ (Romans 8:17)? As the Father's child, you are a recipient and beneficiary of all that belongs to Jesus—what belongs to Him belongs to you. And again, this inheritance is "imperishable, undefiled, and unfading" (1 Peter 1:4 ESV). How is our inheritance imperishable? Because our Savior is imperishable. Why is it undefiled? Because our Savior is the pure, spotless, and blameless Lamb of God. Why is it unfading? Because our Savior is the Light of the World, He never flickers, He never fades. Inheritances are typically secured when someone dies, and our Savior did for those He loved. But our inheritance is unique because it has been sealed through His resurrection (v. 3). Furthermore, our inheritance, Peter wrote, is "reserved in heaven for you" (v. 4). Did you know that if you're a Christian, your name is recorded in heaven? Jesus said, "Rejoice that your names are recorded in heaven" (Luke 10:20). You have a place in glory. You're not going to be a *guest*; you will be a permanent resident. I was recently talking with a woman in my congregation—she has cancer and the doctors told her she is dying. We tried to encourage her, but she ended up encouraging us instead. She said, "I can't wait to go home." What faith! Do you ever think that way? Do you ever say, "I can't wait to go home"?

4. Our heavenly reward is there: gratitude and love are the primary catalysts of living for Christ, but so is the reward promised to those who obey and honor their Father while they are on the earth. Why did Moses obey? Hebrews 11:26 tells us that he was looking forward "to the reward." Why did Abraham obey? Hebrews 11:10 tells us, "He was looking for the city which has foundations, whose architect and builder is God." The same motivation is found throughout the New Testament. Jesus made it clear: "Be glad in that day and leap for joy, for behold, your reward is great in heaven" (Luke 6:23). Believers do not long to transport our earthly treasures to heaven; instead, we "store up" treasures with our Father in heaven (Matthew 6:20). What does this have to do with anxiety? Well, for one, so many people are anxious about the lives they are establishing on earth because they have such a diminished perspective of the reward that awaits them in heaven. If your heart's desire, and chief ambition, was to lay up treasures and rewards in heaven, how would that affect the way you live now?

5. Our greatest joy is heaven. Psalm 16:11 says, "You will make known to me the way of life; in Your presence is fullness of joy; in Your right hand there are pleasures forever." Are the worries of this world dragging you down? God's presence is the fountainhead of joy. Charles Spurgeon said, "The best moment of a Christian's life is his last one, because it is the one that is nearest heaven."[6] The greatest earthly joys do not compare with the joys of heaven. Whatever your view of God may be, it is an incomplete one if it does not include the reality that He is a God of great joy—and in His presence you will experience "fullness of joy; . . . pleasures forever." I can't wait for the day I will hear Jesus say, "Enter into the joy of your master" (Matthew 25:23)!

May I ask you something, as I have asked my own heart? If heaven is your home, why are you so worried about the things of this earth? If your Savior has gone to prepare a place for you in glory, can you not trust Him to provide for all your needs in the here and now?

—————— Reflection Questions ——————

1. What is the good news of God's kingdom for those of us living with worry and anxiety?

2. Why is living life among the family of God so important for the individual Christian? How can you live in a more connected way to the body of Christ?

3. Why does setting our hope on heaven change our perspective here and now? Why do you think we often forget that this world is not our home?

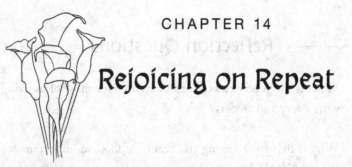

CHAPTER 14

Rejoicing on Repeat

My wife and I recently welcomed our second daughter into the world. She's named after my dad (which is, I confess, unique) and my grandma (who's a legend).

Her name is Scottie Joan.

Seven pounds, seven ounces.

She's beautiful.

Immediately following her delivery, I noticed that she had a large red mark near her eyelid—I asked the doctor what he thought it was, and he replied calmly, "It's just a birthmark." I took his words at face value and didn't really think anything of it. When Scottie was a few weeks old, however, my wife posted a photo of her online and someone wrote her a quick response saying, "That's not a birthmark, that's a hemangioma."

Hemangiomas are fairly common. My sister had one on her back when she was a child—we called it her "strawberry." Interestingly, it was the only way to tell her apart from her twin when they were little.

My wife and I took Scottie to the doctor to get her hemangioma checked out, and to our surprise, the doctor informed us that because of the hemangioma's placement on her eyelid, if left untreated, it would likely blind Scottie in that eye. We asked the doctor, "What can we do?" We were told to start Scottie on a medication immediately in hopes that it would impede the spread of the hemangioma and preserve her vision. To make sure it was safe for Scottie to take the medication, we first had to visit the cardiologist, who would ensure that her heart was stable enough for the medication. At the appointment, the cardiologist informed us that Scottie's hemangioma was merely a symptom of a much more significant underlying disease—a disease that is often linked with a short life expectancy and infant strokes and seizures.

If you're a parent, you can imagine (or have experienced) the worry that fills your heart when you are informed that your seven-pound baby isn't healthy. I said a quick prayer, *God, help me to trust You.*

Shortly after Scottie's diagnosis, she was dropped from insurance.

My chest tightened as I started to dwell on the uncertainties of her health and the costs that may not be covered by insurance. After disputing Scottie's drop from our insurance, I was scheduled to appear before a federal arbitrator who would hear our insurance appeal. One evening, in the middle of our insurance battles, I received a call from my wife at 9:00 p.m. She was on her way home with our two daughters in the car. I answered the phone—she was crying: "Jonny, I need you right now." On her drive home, Caity had smashed into a deer, totaled our car, and broken her elbow. Thankfully, the babies were fine. As I drove her to the ER, I thought, *This all feels like a bad dream.*

In God's providence, sometimes when it rains, it pours.

A week later, I received another urgent call from my wife. She was crying and panicked and said: "It's Scottie! She's hardly breathing, she's unresponsive, and her eyes are rolled back—I can't get her to respond!" I pulled a U-turn and rushed straight to the ER. At one point, I thought she was dead. We were transferred to a children's hospital, where for several days Scottie underwent various tests on her heart, lungs, and brain. We were informed that she had a seizure that had affected her respiratory function. Although there is still a fair amount of unknown with her health, we are thankful she is stable at the moment.

As I write this chapter, we have another appointment scheduled with the neurologist in a few weeks. We are praying that God will protect and preserve our precious baby girl.

Between discussions with doctors and battles with the insurance company, I found myself asking, *Do I truly trust God?*

I'm grateful that, in writing this book, my mind and heart were already steeped in the study of God's character (some would call this coincidence; the believer calls this *providence*). I'm also thankful and I rest in the reality that although I love my daughter immensely, my heavenly Father loves her more than I ever could. She belongs to Him far more than she belongs to me. There is indeed a unique peace that "surpasses all understanding" that gilds my own heart when I cast all my anxieties onto the Lord (Philippians 4:7 ESV; 1 Peter 5:7).

Rejoice Always

One of the realities that has struck me as my wife and I walk this road with our daughter is that I am commanded not only to trust God but to "consider it all joy" when I encounter any sort of trial in my life (James 1:2). My family and finances are up in the air, I am tempted to be anxious about the unknown, yet Scripture instructs me to "rejoice always" and "give thanks in all circumstances" (1 Thessalonians 5:16–18).

Really?

In all circumstances?

In ER visits? In financial uncertainty? In trial? In sorrow? In pain?

Not every circumstance is conducive to joy, but the imperative in Scripture isn't to rejoice *sometimes*, but to "rejoice always."

I realized, *Rejoicing is not an option to consider but rather a command I must obey.* This recognition is convicting at first, but then it's liberating! Why? Because I know that there is no command in Scripture that is impossible to obey. *God's commandments are His enablings.*[1] Therefore, joy in pain and affliction is not only possible, but it is a promised fruit for all who walk in the Spirit (Galatians 5:22). Our Father not only offers His anxious and weary children a way out of the black pit of despair and anxiety—He offers us hope and joy in Christ Jesus! Scripture also says, "It is better to go to a house of mourning than to go to a house of feasting" (Ecclesiastes 7:2). Jesus Himself was "a man of sorrows and acquainted with grief" (Isaiah 53:3 ESV). And Romans 12:15 tells us to "weep with those who weep." So how do we reconcile these truths with the Bible's instruction to "rejoice always"?

The believer can, amid great turmoil and deep despair, possess inexpressible joy (1 Peter 1:8). The apostle Paul put it this way by saying we are "sorrowful yet always rejoicing" (2 Corinthians 6:10). Joy is much different from the conventional understanding of happiness. The English word *happiness* is rooted in the Latin *hap*, which is "chance." Happiness is grounded in *happenings* and *happenstance*. Happiness is a fleeting feeling that is fostered as a spontaneous response to pleasures, successes, situations, and possessions. Joy, however, is distinguished from happiness as it is not dependent on our circumstances but is the conviction that shapes our every attitude toward our circumstances. The Christian's joy is not the *natural* response to life's events but the *supernatural* fruit of believing the gospel of Jesus Christ and the character of our heavenly Father. Christian joy is not something we can manufacture; it is produced in us by the Spirit of God even amid great suffering and pain. Unlike happiness, joy is grounded in our faith and the changeless character of our heavenly Father. When we look at our circumstances, our happiness will inevitably wane, but when we fix our gaze on God, He gives us both peace and indescribable joy.

Joy in Suffering

The apostle Peter's first epistle was written to a church community that endured much persecution and affliction. The notorious emperor Nero would often crucify followers of Jesus; at other times, he would feed them to the lions in the Colosseum; sometimes he would light them on fire and use them as human torches in his gardens. Nero was ruthless. Nevertheless, in spite of the persecution and pain, Peter began his epistle by saying, "In this you greatly *rejoice*, even though now for a little while, if necessary, you have been distressed by various trials" (1 Peter 1:6, emphasis added). Peter continued by saying, "To the degree that you share the sufferings of Christ, keep on rejoicing" (1 Peter 4:13). Peter didn't merely tell them to "trust God"—he went one step further—he told them to rejoice and to keep on rejoicing.

Have you ever considered your trials in this light? Do you *rejoice* in the midst of pain, affliction, trial, and trouble?

The apostle Paul expressed a similar exhortation when he wrote to the Philippian church. Paul wrote this letter while imprisoned, and seventeen times throughout his short epistle he mentioned joy. While chained to his Roman guard, Paul said, "Rejoice in the Lord always; again I will say, rejoice!" (Philippians 4:4). Earlier, in Philippians 2, he said, "Even if I am being poured out as a drink offering upon the sacrifice and service of your faith, I rejoice and share my joy with you all" (v. 17). Paul was saying, *Even if I die tomorrow in Nero's dungeon, I rejoice!* Not only that, but he also added, "I urge you, rejoice in the same way and share your joy with me" (v. 18). Paul continued, "Finally, my brethren, rejoice in the Lord" (3:1). Paul's joy was unshakable. Why? Not because he found joy in himself, but because his joy was "in the Lord." What gave Paul such a level of joy? I believe the answer is found in some of the other key words he employed throughout his letter: ten times throughout the book of Philippians, Paul referred to "the mind"; five times he referred to our thoughts; and once he compelled his readers to "remember." What was the secret to Paul's joy? His mind was anchored in the character of God. Paul said in Philippians 4:8 (ESV), "Finally, brothers, whatever is true, whatever is honorable, whatever is just, whatever is pure, whatever is lovely, whatever is commendable, if there is any excellence, if there is anything worthy of praise, think about these things." True joy is never found by looking at circumstances; it is found by looking to our Father.

Both Peter's and Paul's exhortations to rejoice sound reminiscent of the words of Jesus in His Sermon on the Mount: "Blessed are you when people insult you and persecute you, and falsely say all kinds of evil against you because of Me. *Rejoice and be glad*, for your reward in heaven is great" (Matthew 5:11–12, emphasis added). Did you catch that? Jesus said to "rejoice and be glad." In Luke's Gospel, Jesus instructed those who were ostracized, alienated, and insulted to "leap for joy." Why? "For behold, your reward is great in heaven" (Luke 6:23).

James, the half brother of Jesus, wrote his epistle to the churches that had been scattered due to the persecution inflicted by Herod Agrippa. After his customary greeting, James began his epistle by saying, "Consider it all joy, my brethren, when you encounter various trials" (James 1:2). The first thing James told the scattered, dispersed, and persecuted Christians was to consider every trial a catalyst for joy. He essentially said, *You should be happier about your trials than you are about your blessings.* Why? Because the "testing of your faith produces endurance" (v. 3). Trials aren't naturally conducive to joy, yet the believer reckons them all joy for a few reasons:

1. The believer knows that trials are refining fire in which we are conformed to the image of Christ (James 1:2; 1 Peter 1:7). Isn't this your chief ambition as a Christian? Don't you want to be like your Savior? God uses trials in our lives to make us more like Jesus—therefore, we consider trials all joy.

2. The believer can find joy in trials because the distresses of this life prepare us for the joys of the next. As Jesus said, "Rejoice and be glad, for your reward in heaven is great" (Matthew 5:12). Every tear we cry is a reminder that we were not made for this world—but for another one to come.

3. Our perseverance through trials is one of the proofs of saving faith. After Peter detailed that believers are to rejoice in trials, he then explained why: "So that the proof of your faith, being more precious than gold which is perishable, even though tested by fire, may be found to result in praise and glory and honor at the revelation of Jesus Christ" (1 Peter 1:7). Remember how we observed that a genuine Christian can never lose salvation? That's our security. But our confidence in our security, our assurance, can wane; the devil seeks to antagonize and accuse—he promotes doubt and despair in our hearts and minds, so we lose all hope and certainty of our adoption in Christ. Yet Scripture teaches us that the trials and troubles we face serve as the confirmation and validation of God's work in our lives.

In God's design for our trials, there is a real place to mourn, grieve, and express sorrow. But the believer's sorrow differs from the world's because only those who trust in Christ can be "sorrowful yet always rejoicing" (2 Corinthians 6:10). To rejoice in great sorrow is easier said than done; however, because it is a command in Scripture, we can know with certainty that it is possible for us to obey. Why? Because, once again, *God's commands are His enablings.* This means that God does not merely tell us to have joy; He gives us ample—nay, overwhelming—reasons to rejoice in every circumstance. When we run to the world as the source of joy, we find it to be a dead well, but when we run to our Father, we find Him to be an everlasting fountain and spring of supernatural joy.

Sources of Joy

Your Father's Character

Joy is the proper response to the character of our heavenly Father. Because I know that my God is sovereign, wise, loving, and all powerful, and He is determined to bless me as His child, I possess a deep-seated confidence, not only in His control, but in His plan. Knowing that my Father is working everything out for my good and His glory cultivates a joy that the world does not understand. Do you grasp that God wants the best for you? I cannot always rejoice in my circumstances, but God's Spirit enables me to rejoice in the God who controls my circumstances. The believer's joy is impenetrable and unflagging because it is anchored not in fleeting circumstance but in our Father's changeless and constant character. Who He is gives us joy. Do you, like Paul, dwell on the character of God? Do you think about all that is lovely, noble, and excellent about Him and His kingdom (Philippians 4:8)? If you do, you will draw near to God, not as a subject, but as a child of your Father. You will experience intimacy and fellowship with Him, and, consequently, you will be able to say with the psalmist, "In Your presence is fullness of joy" (Psalm 16:11).

The Word of God

The joy of the Lord abides only in those who abide in His Word. Psalm 19:8 says, "The precepts of the LORD are right, rejoicing the heart." True joy can be gleaned only by those who mine the gold of God's Word. You cannot rest confidently in the character of God if you do not saturate your mind and heart with His truth. Without the Word of God, you are a stranger to His promises, and, in consequence, you will be a stranger to unassailable joy. But in God's Word we remember who He is, we recall what He has done and is doing, and our hopes are lifted from the things of this world and directed toward the one to come.

In Jesus' final words to His disciples, He said, "These things I have spoken to you so that My joy may be in you, and that your joy may be made full" (John 15:11). Isn't that amazing? Jesus intends for His joy to be in you. How? How can we have the joy of Jesus? Well, the only way is for the Spirit of God to take the Word of God and instill in us the joy that can only come from God. Paul said in Romans 15:4, "Whatever was written in earlier times was written for our instruction, so that through perseverance and the encouragement of the Scriptures we might have hope." The Christian is promised pain, difficulty (John 16:33), and persecution (2 Timothy 3:12), yet we are commanded to rejoice always, because in God's Word we read of God's promises, and in the greatest storms we find the worth of the anchor that is Christ Jesus. The stories of Peter's joy in the face of persecution and the account of Paul's joy in a Roman dungeon serve a divine purpose—to give you hope (Romans 15:4).

The Gospel

Can you say this with an honest heart?

If I never receive another blessing outside of what I have already received in Christ, I would still have overwhelming reasons to rejoice.

Repeatedly throughout the New Testament, and specifically

in Paul's writing, we read the phrase "in Christ," "in Christ," "in Christ." Paul did not say simply to rejoice, he said to "rejoice in the Lord" (Philippians 4:4). Can I point out something that may be rather obvious? You cannot rejoice in Jesus if you have not placed your faith in Him. But to those who know Him as Savior, there is a deep-seated joy that comes from knowing that our greatest need in life has already been met—*our sins are forgiven!* And because I am "in Christ," Christ's joy is always in me. Joy is not something I muster up—it's a fruit of the Spirit that lives within me. If you are anxious, worried, or despairing, it is an exercise in futility to attempt to produce joy in and of yourself; you must abide in Christ to abide in His joy (John 15:4–9). True peace and true joy are not the absence of uncertainty, pain, and difficulty but the presence of Jesus in your life. The only people who can say "The joy of the LORD is [my] strength" (Nehemiah 8:10 ESV) are those who can say, "Jesus is my Savior!"

Your Future Inheritance

The apostle Paul's biography includes almost unthinkable and unbearable suffering. He was given thirty-nine lashes (five times), beaten with rods (three times), shipwrecked (three times), stoned nearly to death, beaten, abandoned, betrayed, and imprisoned, yet he said, "Therefore we do not lose heart, but though our outer man is decaying, yet our inner man is being renewed day by day. For momentary, light affliction is producing for us an eternal weight of glory far beyond all comparison" (2 Corinthians 4:16–17). Paul had fixed his hope on his eternal inheritance. Every ounce of suffering in Paul's mind paled in comparison with the joy he would experience in the presence of the Lord (Philippians 1:23). Jesus provides similar hope and joy to those of us who face anxieties and affliction in this life: "Rejoice and be glad, for your reward in heaven is great" (Matthew 5:12). Our future home with our Savior not only gives us hope for the next life but gives us joy in this present one. Paul said in Romans 8:18, "I consider that the sufferings of this present time are not worthy to be compared with the glory that is to be revealed to us." When was the last time you rejoiced at the thought of your future inheritance with Christ? When was the last time you leaped for joy because your name was written in heaven (Luke 6:23)? Know this: whenever you lose sight of heaven in your thinking, you can be sure you will lose joy in your heart.

This world was never meant to satisfy and was never intended to fulfill. We are, as C. S. Lewis used to say, "made for another world,"[2] and fixing our hope on the world to come is what sustains our joy and anchors our hope. This world is our temporary home, we are just passing through, our destination and secure destiny is in glory with Christ. Therefore, we cling to the exhortation to "walk by faith, not by sight" (2 Corinthians 5:7).

> Now may the God of hope fill you with all *joy* and peace in believing, so that you will abound in hope by the power of the Holy Spirit. (Romans 15:13, emphasis added)

Joy is one of the spiritual birthmarks of the Christian, but it must be understood: joy isn't the absence of sadness—it's the presence of God's Holy Spirit in our lives. Joy is more about our perspective than it is our circumstances. Can I point out one final thing? Humility is not only the logical response to our God who has revealed Himself in His Word; it is also a prerequisite to lasting and impenetrable joy. Why? Because in order to find joy in the Lord we must first take our eyes off ourselves and fix them on Christ, "the author and perfecter of our faith" (Hebrews 12:2) and the One who will one day soon bring us home. First Peter 5:6–7 reads, "Humble yourselves under the mighty hand of God . . . casting all your anxiety on Him, because He cares for you."

Do you know your Father's character? Do you trust in His love, sovereignty, wisdom, presence, and power in your life? It's one thing to consider these truths, it's an entirely different thing to come and bow down before Him in humility and cast your anxieties on Him. You can trust your Father—*He cares for you.*

Jesus bids His followers to consider the lilies. Why? Because if God cares for the flowers, how much more does He care for you? We live in an anxious world, and every individual is asking, Where can peace be found? There is only one answer: supernatural peace is only received by those who come to God's supernatural Word and meditate deeply upon His loving and changeless character.

I close this book with the verse with which we began:

> The steadfast of mind You will keep in perfect peace,
> Because he trusts in You.
> Trust in the LORD forever,
> For in GOD the LORD, we have an everlasting Rock.
>
> Isaiah 26:3–4

Reflection Questions

1. Charles Spurgeon said that God's commandments are His enablings. In this light, how does the knowledge that God bids His people to "rejoice always" provide us with hope (Philippians 4:4)?

2. Read James 1:2. Why can the believer have joy even during difficult trials? What does it look like to be sorrowful and yet rejoicing?

3. How can God's character be a source of joy? In a world of increasing anxiety, how can the revelation of God's goodness and love produce liberating peace in your life?

Acknowledgments

First Thessalonians 5:16–18 says, "Rejoice always; pray without ceasing; in everything give thanks; for this is God's will for you in Christ Jesus." Gratitude is not only the logical response of the redeemed, it is the *will of God for our life*. As I consider all the people that the Lord has put in my life, I want to take a moment to express my gratitude for a select few—especially as it relates to this book.

To my family: Caity Jean, every ministerial endeavor that I do is impossible without your partnership, love, and support. You encourage, challenge, and sharpen me. Outside of Christ, you are God's greatest gift to me. Dad, thanks for raising me in a home that lifted high the Word of God. Mom, thank you for teaching us to memorize Scripture at a young age and for your keen editorial eye throughout this process.

To the elders and church family at Stonebridge Bible Church: Much of what is written here is the fruit of the first preaching series I did in the Psalms. Your love for God's Word and for the person of Jesus Christ makes me so grateful to be your pastor. I'm excited for what God has in store for our church!

To my friends: Costi, thanks for encouraging me to write. Erik

Acknowledgments

Wolgemuth, thank you for working so faithfully with me on this project as my agent. Harry Walls, thanks for . . . everything.

Dr. Horner, thanks for your Bible reading plan—life-changing. Erik Thoennes, thanks for fueling my love for the character of God (I'm so grateful for our conversations at Hume Lake).

To my spiritual mentors: I never met R. C. Sproul, but it would be difficult to minimize the magnitude of his impact on me. Thank you, Sinclair Ferguson, for the way you preach and teach; Pastor John MacArthur, for your commitment to God's Word; Jerry Bridges, for the way you combine conviction with tenderness and compassion; and Joel Beeke, for your "experiential" preaching.

To the Zondervan team—thanks in particular to my editor Paul Pastor (and Dirk Buursma), for your sharp editorial observations and how you helped me communicate the truth of God's character in a way that is both powerful and tender.

Ultimately, I want to thank God for saving me and extending to me the opportunity to write about His glorious character. What a privilege it is to study the Bible, preach the Bible, and, here, write a book that reflects the great truths we find *in the Bible*.

Notes

Introduction

1. D. Martyn Lloyd-Jones, *Spiritual Depression: Its Causes and Its Cure* (1965; repr., Grand Rapids: Zondervan, 1998), 19.

Chapter 1: Earth: A Painful and Confusing Place

1. Ryan Prior, "1 in 4 Young People Are Reporting Suicidal Thoughts. Here's How to Help," CNN Health, August 15, 2020, www .cnn.com/2020/08/14/health/young-people-suicidal-ideation -wellness/index.html; "Teen Anxiety Statistics Are on the Rise— How Can You Help Your Teen?," Newport Academy, April 29, 2020, www.newportacademy.com/resources/mental-health /teen-anxiety-statistics.

2. Robert Leahy, "How Big a Problem Is Anxiety?," *Psychology Today*, April 30, 2008, www.psychologytoday.com/us/blog /anxiety-files/200804/how-big-problem-is-anxiety.

3. Throughout this book I often link anxiety, fear, and melancholy (or depression), not only because Scripture does (as we will soon discover), but also because modern psychology does. As psychologist and author Jean Twenge noted, "Anxiety tends to predispose people to depression" ("The Age of Anxiety? Birth Cohort Change in Anxiety and Neuroticism, 1952–1993," *Journal of Personality and*

Social Psychology 79, no. 6 [2000]: 1018, www.apa.org/pubs
/journals/releases/psp7961007.pdf). Anxiety and depression are
typically adjoining afflictions. One tends to lead to the other.

4. See Jeff Cunningham, "Why Is Generation Z So Depressed—
Overprotective Parents," Thunderbird School of Global
Management, October 22, 2018, https://thunderbird.asu.edu
/thought-leadership/insights/why-generation-z-so-depressed
-overprotective-parents.

5. See Debra J. Brody and Qiuping Gu, "Antidepressant Use among
Adults: United States 2015–2018," National Center for Health
Statistics, September 2020, www.cdc.gov/nchs/products/databriefs
/db377.htm.

6. See "Older Women Use the Most Antidepressants, Survey Finds,"
Women's Healthcare, www.npwomenshealthcare.com/older
-women-use-the-most-antidepressants-survey-finds, accessed
April 5, 2024.

7. I first realized this when reading Jerry Bridges's book *Trusting God*
(1988; repr., Colorado Springs: NavPress, 2016). The influence of
his book on my life and on the content of *Consider the Lilies* cannot
be overstated.

8. "Anxiety Disorders," National Alliance on Mental Illness,
December 2017, www.nami.org/About-Mental-Illness
/Mental-Health-Conditions/Anxiety-Disorders.

9. Emily Croot, "The Financial Costs of Anxiety," Thrive Global,
October 1, 2019, https://community.thriveglobal.com
/the-financial-costs-of-anxiety.

10. Kai Wright, *The United States of Anxiety* podcast, *The Nation*,
accessed April 5, 2024, www.thenation.com/content
/united-states-of-anxiety.

11. Paraphrased from Bridges, *Trusting God*, 4.

12. J. I. Packer, *Knowing God* (Downers Grove, IL: InterVarsity, 1973),
19.

Chapter 2: Perfect Peace?

1. Charles Spurgeon, "The Cause and Cure of a Wounded Spirit," sermon, *Metropolitan Tabernacle Pulpit*, vol. 42, April 16, 1885, www.spurgeon.org/resource-library/sermons/the-cause-and-cure-of-a-wounded-spirit.
2. A. W. Tozer, *The Knowledge of the Holy* (1961; repr., San Francisco: HarperSanFrancisco, 1992), 4.

Chapter 3: Embodied Beings

1. A. W. Tozer, *Of God and Men: Cultivating the Divine/Human Relationship* (Chicago: Moody Press, 2015), 77.
2. D. Martyn Lloyd-Jones, *Spiritual Depression: Its Causes and Its Cure* (1965; repr., Grand Rapids: Zondervan, 1998), 15.
3. Lloyd-Jones, *Spiritual Depression*, 16.
4. Lloyd-Jones, *Spiritual Depression*, 19.
5. Charles Spurgeon, "The Secret of Happiness," No. 3277, A Sermon Published on Thursday, December 8, 1910, Christian Classics Ethereal Library, https://ccel.org/ccel/spurgeon/sermons56/sermons56.l.html.
6. Charles Spurgeon, "Great Mercies," in *The Sword and the Trowel* (London: Passmore & Alabaster, 1871), 323.

Chapter 4: The Spiritual Physician

1. Corrie ten Boom, *God Is My Hiding Place: 40 Devotions for Refuge and Strength* (Grand Rapids: Chosen, 2021), 38.
2. D. Martyn Lloyd-Jones, *Studies in the Sermon on the Mount* (1959; repr., Grand Rapids: Wm. B. Eerdmans, 2000), 353.
3. Lloyd-Jones, *Sermon on the Mount*, 361.
4. Lloyd-Jones, *Sermon on the Mount*, 367.
5. Josh Howarth, "Alarming Average Screen Time Statistics (2024)," Exploding Topics, December 4, 2023, https://explodingtopics.com/blog/screen-time-stats.
6. Christinia Camilleri, Justin T. Perry, and Stephen Sammut, "Compulsive Internet Pornography Use and Mental Health: A

Cross-Sectional Study in a Sample of University Students in the United States," *Frontiers in Psychology* 11 (January 12, 2021), https://doi.org/10.3389/fpsyg.2020.613244.

Chapter 5: Your Mind Matters

1. Emphasis added to the Bible quotations in this list.
2. Thomas Watson, "Meditation," in *Extracts from the Writings of Thomas Watson* (Cheshire: Scripture Truth, 2009), 73.
3. See Oswald Chambers, *Studies in the Sermon on the Mount* (London: Simpkin Marshall, 1948), 50.
4. David Saxton, *God's Battle Plan for the Mind: The Puritan Practice of Biblical Meditation* (Grand Rapids: Reformation Heritage, 2015), 4. This book has been critically important for this section. I highly recommend it.
5. Corrie ten Boom, *Don't Wrestle, Just Nestle* (Old Tappan, NJ: Revell, 1978), 33.

Chapter 6: Knowing *Abba*

1. J. I. Packer, *Knowing God* (1973; repr., Downers Grove, IL: InterVarsity, 1993), 200.
2. Packer, *Knowing God*, 201.
3. D. Martyn Lloyd-Jones, *Spiritual Depression: Its Causes and Its Cure* (1965; repr., Grand Rapids: Zondervan, 1998), 27.
4. Lloyd-Jones, *Spiritual Depression*, 28.
5. Lloyd-Jones, *Spiritual Depression*, 28.
6. Burk Parsons, "The Fear of the Lord," *Tabletalk*, January 2018, https://tabletalkmagazine.com/article/2018/01/the-fear-of-the-lord.
7. This is often attributed to Jonathan Edwards and Philip Melanchthon, although there is no direct source.
8. Packer, *Knowing God*, 195.
9. Lloyd-Jones, *Spiritual Depression*, 35.
10. Ephesians 2:4–5.
11. Packer, *Knowing God*, 195.

Chapter 7: Forever Himself, Forever Good

1. John Calvin, *Institutes*, I.1.i.
2. Sinclair Ferguson, "I Am Who I Am," *Things Unseen* podcast, February 27, 2024, www.ligonier.org/podcasts/things-unseen -with-sinclair-ferguson/i-am-who-i-am.
3. Augustine is reported to have said that the Bible is shallow enough for a child not to drown, yet deep enough for an elephant to swim.

Chapter 8: Infinite Understanding

1. A. W. Tozer, *The Knowledge of the Holy* (1961; repr., San Francisco: HarperSanFrancisco, 1992), 1.
2. Elizabeth Howell and Ailsa Harvey, "How Many Stars Are in the Universe?," Space.com, February 11, 2022, www.space.com/26078 -how-many-stars-are-there.html.
3. Lizzy McNeill, "How Many Animals Are Born in the World Every Day?," BBC, June 10, 2018, www.bbc.com/news/science -environment-44412495.
4. "Global Dashboard," The Joshua Project, https://joshuaproject.net, accessed May 3, 2024.
5. Augustine, *Confessions*, trans. J. G. Pilkington, Logos, www .logoslibrary.org/augustine/confessions/0404.html, accessed May 3, 2024.
6. Quoted in Martin H. Manser, *The Westminster Collection of Christian Quotes* (Louisville, KY: Westminster John Knox, 2001), 26.
7. J. I. Packer, *Knowing God* (Downers Grove, IL: InterVarsity, 1973), 42.

Chapter 9: Above All

1. Quoted in John Brown, *John Bunyan: His Life, Times, and Work* (New York: Hulbert, 1928), 224.
2. John Bunyan, *Grace Abounding to the Chief of Sinners* (Oxford: Clarendon, 1962), 98.
3. "North Korea Says It Tested Underwater Nuclear Attack Drone,"

CBS News, updated January 19, 2024, www.cbsnews.com/news/north-korea-underwater-nuclear-weapon-system-test.

4. Jerry Bridges, *Trusting God* (1988; repr., Colorado Springs: NavPress, 2016), 37.

5. Margaret Clarkson, *Destined for Glory* (Grand Rapids: Eerdmans, 1983), vii.

6. Margaret Clarkson, *Grace Grows Best in Winter* (Grand Rapids: Eerdmans, 1984), 40–41.

7. Clarkson, *Grace Grows*, 21.

8. John Piper goes into detail on this reality in his sermon "Ten Aspects of God's Sovereignty over Suffering and Satan's Hand in It," Desiring God National Conference, October 7, 2005, Minneapolis, www.desiringgod.org/messages/ten-aspects-of-gods-sovereignty-over-suffering-and-satans-hand-in-it.

9. I am indebted to a conversation I had with Scott Christensen, author of *What about Evil? A Defense of God's Sovereign Glory* (Phillipsburg, PA: P&R, 2020) for his help in thinking through this chapter.

10. John Piper, "Where Is God? The Supremacy of Christ in an Age of Terror," Desiring God, September 11, 2005, www.desiringgod.org/messages/where-is-god.

11. For more on God's sovereignty and human evil, read Scott Christensen, *Defeating Evil: How God Glorifies Himself in a Dark World* (Phillipsburg, NJ: P&R, 2024), 15, 106.

12. Once again I find myself indebted to Jerry Bridges and his book *Trusting God.* I had experienced firsthand the glib expressions of God's people, but Bridges, as he always does, articulates so clearly the reality I was grappling with. His writing has changed my life.

13. Elisabeth Elliot, *Suffering Is Never for Nothing* (Nashville: B&H, 2019).

14. C. S. Lewis, *The Problem of Pain* (1940; repr., San Francisco: HarperSanFrancisco, 2001), 91.

15. "Grant Colfax Tullar," Hymnary.org, https://hymnary.org/person/Tullar_Grant, accessed May 3, 2024.

Chapter 10: Lavish Love

1. "More Americans Plan to Buy Gifts for Their Pets Than In-Laws, According to New Survey on Holiday Spending," PR Newswire, December 5, 2022, www.prnewswire.com/news-releases/more-americans-plan-to-buy-gifts-for-their-pets-than-in-laws-according-to-new-survey-on-holiday-spending-301692875.html.
2. I again find myself indebted to Jerry Bridges for helping put to words what has often been so true in my own life.
3. I'll never forget watching R. C. Sproul teach on this reality in his Ligonier teaching series. Life-changing.
4. Personal communication.
5. Psalm 32:1.
6. John Piper, "How to Experience the Outpouring of God's Love," Desiring God, May 1, 2016, www.desiringgod.org/messages/how-to-experience-the-outpouring-of-gods-love.
7. Charles Spurgeon, *The Treasury of David: Spurgeon's Classic Work on the Psalms* (Grand Rapids: Kregel Academic, 1976), 378.

Chapter 11: Our Present Refuge

1. 2 Kings 18:29–30, 33, 35.
2. I heard Dr. Joel Beeke say this in a sermon.
3. Martyn Lloyd-Jones, *Spiritual Depression* (Grand Rapids: Zondervan, 1988), 143.
4. Elisabeth Elliot once said, "In the first shock of death everything that has seemed most dependable had given way. Mountains were falling, the earth was reeling. In such a time it is a profound comfort to know that although all things seem to be shaken, one thing is not: God is not shaken" (*Facing the Death of Someone You Love* [Westchester, IL: Good News, 1980], 8).

Chapter 12: The One Who Hears

1. Quoted in Ashton Oxenden, *Fervent Prayer* (London: Hatchard, 1861), 186.

2. Corrie ten Boom, *I Stand at the Door and Knock* (Grand Rapids: Zondervan, 2008), 115.

3. John Calvin, *Institutes of the Christian Religion*, vol. 2, ed. John T. McNeill (Philadelphia: Westminster, 1960), 865.

4. J. I. Packer, quoted in Kevin DeYoung, *The Lord's Prayer: Learning from Jesus on What, Why, and How to Pray* (Wheaton, IL: Crossway, 2022), 34.

5. "Daily Devotionals: Morning and Evening with A. W. Tozer," Study Light.org, January 11, www.studylight.org/daily-devotionals/eng /toz.html, accessed May 3, 2024.

6. George Müller, *The Autobiography of George Müller* (New Kensington, PA: Whitaker House, 1984), 42.

7. Margaret Clarkson, "Singleness: His Share for Me," *Christianity Today*, February 1979, 14–15.

8. H. B. Charles Jr., "The Believer's Secret Weapon: Ephesians 6:18," H. B. Charles Jr. website, https://hbcharlesjr.com/resource-library /sermon-outlines/the-believers-secret-weapon-ephesians-618, accessed May 3, 2024.

9. J. C. Ryle, *Practical Religion* (n.p.: Lulu, 2018), 86.

10. Müller, *Autobiography*, 138–39.

11. John Bunyan, *The Complete Works of John Bunyan* (Philadelphia: Bradley, Garretson, 1872), 80.

Chapter 13: Mission, Family, Future

1. Joni Eareckson Tada, "Broken to Comfort the Broken: How Quadriplegia Prepared Me to Carry Others," Desiring God, April 20, 2020, www.desiringgod.org/articles /broken-to-comfort-the-broken.

2. Joni Eareckson Tada, "I Sing My Way through Pain: Three Lessons in Resilient Joy," Desiring God, February 28, 2023, www.desiringgod.org/articles/i-sing-my-way-through-pain.

3. See Elisabeth Elliot, *Suffering Is Never for Nothing* (Nashville: B&H, 2019).

4. Quoted in Justin Taylor, "Do the Next Thing," The Gospel Coalition, October 25, 2017, www.thegospelcoalition.org/blogs/justin-taylor/do-the-next-thing.
5. J. C. Ryle, "Heaven," https://thirdmill.org/articles/jc_ryle/jc_ryle.Heaven.html, accessed May 3, 2024.
6. Charles Spurgeon, "Foretastes of the Heavenly Life," in *Sermons of the Rev. C. H. Spurgeon* (New York: Sheldon & Blakeman, 1858), 136.

Chapter 14: Rejoicing on Repeat

1. Charles Spurgeon, "Impotence and Omnipotence," *Metropolitan Tabernacle Pulpit*, vol. 38, February 16, 1890, www.spurgeon.org/resource-library/sermons/impotence-and-omnipotence.
2. C. S. Lewis, *Mere Christianity* (San Francisco: HarperOne, 2001), 137.